GIRLS
WITH
SWORDS

HOW TO CARRY YOUR CROSS
LIKE A HERO

FENCING
MANUAL

LISA BEVERE

Girls with Swords Fencing Manual
Copyright © 2013 by Messenger International

PUBLISHED BY MESSENGER INTERNATIONAL
P.O. Box 888
Palmer Lake, CO 80133-0888

Unless otherwise indicated, all Scripture quotations are from The Holy Bible, English Standard Version® (ESV®), copyright © 2001 by Crossway, a publishing ministry of Good News Publishers. Used by permission. All rights reserved. Scripture quotations marked The Message or (MSG) are taken from THE MESSAGE. Copyright © 1993, 1994, 1995, 1996, 2000, 2001, 2002. Used by permission of NavPress Publishing Group. Scripture quotations marked (NLT) are taken from the Holy Bible, New Living Translation, copyright © 1996, 2004, 2007 by Tyndale House Foundation. Used by permission of Tyndale House Publishers, Inc., Carol Stream, Illinois 60188. All rights reserved. Scripture quotations marked (ASV) are taken from the American Standard Version. Scripture quotations marked (KJV) are taken from the King James Version. Scripture quotations marked (NIV) are taken from the Holy Bible, New International Version®, NIV®. Copyright © 1973, 1978, 1984, 2011 by Biblica, Inc.™ Used by permission of Zondervan. All rights reserved worldwide. www.zondervan.com The "NIV" and "New International Version" are trademarks registered in the United States Patent and Trademark Office by Biblica, Inc.™

Some use of *italics* and **bold** treatment in Scripture and leader quotes indicates the author's added emphasis. Some uses of brackets indicate the author's parenthetical insertions.

Special sword illustrations in chapters 5-6, 9-13 by Allan Nygren
Hand-lettered illustrations by Andrea Howey

SPECIAL SALES
Pastors, churches, and ministry leaders can receive special discounts when purchasing Messenger International resources. For information, please visit MessengerInternational.org or call 1-800-648-1477.

COVER, DESIGN & PRINT PRODUCTION:
The Eastco Group
3646 California Rd.
Orchard Park, NY 14127
www.theeastcogroup.com

Designer: Heather Huether

Printed in Canada

CONTENTS

Lovely Brave One,

I'm so excited you have chosen to go a bit deeper with *Girls with Swords* and decided to work your way through the *Fencing Manual*. To fully understand my excitement, you need to know the backstory—why it is so important that you are not only a girl with a sword, but perhaps one who will choose to go on and wield her sword with extraordinary finesse. This story stretches back to my last book, *Lioness Arising.*

Lioness Arising had been out for two months, and since the moment of its release, my life had been a bit of an international blur. So I did an after-the-fact prayer asking for confirmation. It went something like, "God, I know I was supposed to preach *Lioness Arising* as a message. I hope it was okay that I wrote it as a book. I would really love a confirmation from You on that."

The book was already in five languages! But I know that God knows me, and He knows how to work with me even in all my randomness.

Later that night, I was home with my boys and in the throes of a school project with my youngest son. We had just assembled all the components we needed when John called from the East Coast.

I want to give you a window into life with my husband. We have been married for more than thirty years. Wives, if your husband has a habit you find annoying and he's been doing it for thirty years, you might as well just call it cute. So in light of this, my husband has a cute, at times annoying habit of calling to put me on the phone with complete strangers. He gets me on the line and says, "Hey, honey, I have a guy you will want to talk to!"

That night I countered, "Actually, I don't want to talk to anyone tonight, John. I'm in the middle of a school project."

John assured me, "No, no, you're going to want to talk to this guy. I gave him your number. Get ready; he's going to call you."

I was a bit frustrated when the phone rang about five minutes later. I offered a pitiful, "Hello."

He said, "Is this Lisa Bevere?"

I said, "Yes."

He said, "Ma'am, your husband held up your book tonight—*Lioness Arising*—and he said that lions are the best killers, but lionesses are better hunters."

I said, "Well, of course he would say that. That's actually all he knows because he hasn't read the book."

Undaunted, he continued, "Well, I am calling you to tell you *why* your book is important. Because you are right—lionesses are better hunters." All of a sudden he had my full attention. He said, "Let me tell you what I do here at Fort Bragg. I work with special operations. Are you aware we are not winning the war in Afghanistan?"

As a resident of Colorado Springs, I regularly flew with men enlisted in the Air Force or the Army seated beside me on planes. I had the opportunity to speak with many of them, specifically about the war in Afghanistan. I responded, "Yes, I am aware."

He continued, "Do you want to know one of the reasons why we are not winning this war?"

I thought to myself, *Yes, in the middle of my son's school project, I want to know why the US military is not winning this war!* But I simply replied, "Why?"

He said, "Their culture forbids our men to speak to their women. If you can't speak to the women, you can't flip the culture; and if you can't flip the culture, you can't win the war.

"So now, in addition to teams of special operations men, we have created a team of women. These women will speak with the Afghan women and tell them they have voice and value. They will share with them how democracy will serve both their sons and daughters better. They will take care of their minor medical needs and deliver their babies."

I was intrigued but still unsure why we were talking. He continued, "I need to tell you the name of this group. They're called Team Lioness, and they're about to be deployed. May I have a copy of your book for each of them?" The moment was such a profound confirmation for me that I almost fainted.

I tell you this story for one very important reason: If the US military understands that *without the involvement of women, we can fight but we will never win*, it is time we as a Church get on board. The men need us to come alongside them so that the Church of Jesus Christ can win. We need women who will fight alongside the men, not fight with the men. It is not good for men to be without us. When God created man and woman, He declared that *together*, they were excellent in every way.

I believe that the Church is waiting for the women to rise up involved, armed, trained, prepared, and celebrated. Rather than arguing for your rights, why not argue with your life? Let's live in such a compelling way that the men want us involved. I don't believe it is any accident that all God's children (male and female) have been entrusted with a sword, and that fencing is one of the sports in which women hold their own right alongside the men. *Lioness Arising* was a wake-up call; *Girls with Swords* is your armory.

You are needed in this fight. *En garde*!

―――― ∞∞∞ ――――

Suggestions for Use

This *Fencing Manual* contains fourteen chapters, which correspond with the fourteen book chapters and the eight teaching sessions.

If you are using the video sessions:
Read the chapter(s) in the *Girls with Swords* book, complete the chapter(s) in this *Fencing Manual*, and watch the corresponding DVD session—in that order.

The first time your group meets, watch the "Week 1 Welcome" on the first DVD. This will position your group for the week one reading (chapters one in the book and *Fencing Manual*). The next time you meet, watch video session one.

Book and Fencing Manual Chapter(s)	Video Session
Chapter 1	Session 1: You Are a Target
Chapter 2	Session 2: A Sword is Born
Chapters 3-4	Session 3: Heroes and Battlegrounds
Chapter 5	Session 4: The Cross as a Sword
Chapters 6-7	Session 5: Forging Warriors and Swords
Chapter 8	Session 6: Sword Words
Chapters 9-13	Session 7: Swords
Chapter 14	Session 8: How to Carry Your Cross Like a Hero

FEATURES TO LOOK FOR IN EACH CHAPTER:

- ⚜ **Scriptures** – profound passages from the Word to transform your life
- ⚜ **Fencing Masters** – words of wisdom from skilled sword bearers
- ⚜ **Sword Play** – activities for you and your sparring partners
- ⚜ **Fencing Lessons** – highlighted "power points" from each chapter
- ⚜ **En Garde** – further identification of your fencing expertise
- ⚜ **Skill Check** – key statements to help you define and develop fencing finesse
- ⚜ **Fencing Facts** – fun and insightful facts about the sport
- ⚜ **Sword Words** – declarations of eternal truth that will shape your world
- ⚜ **Impressions** – your personal reflections
- ⚜ **Discussion Questions** – this symbol (G) denotes questions suggested for group discussion

Throughout the *Fencing Manual*, you will also discover insights from influential leaders. (*Note*: Celebrating one's moments of inspiration and brilliance does not equate to endorsing one's entire life. Pause a moment and lean into the world of a man or woman who has gone before you in time.)

Some helpful pointers...

Begin and end each of your study sessions with prayer. Invite the Holy Spirit to teach you and lead you into all truth (see John 16:13).

Be consistent in your study. Whatever time and place you choose to do the study, stick to it. If you fall behind, don't quit. Push through to the finish. Your efforts will be rewarded.

Be honest as you answer each question. There are no wrong answers except those that are dishonest. Knowing the truth of God's Word, along with the truth about yourself, will bring freedom to your life that can be found no other way.

The material contained in this *Fencing Manual* is life-transforming because it is the Word of God. It will change and challenge you to the degree you allow it. It is my prayer that on this training ground, you will learn to speak heaven's words, shoulder your cross, and become a sword in our Savior's hand.

Most Sincerely,

Lisa

You Are a Target

Welcome to this epic battle, my warrior sister.

Sadly our earth is presently a war zone without any neutral territory. For this very reason our wise God and heavenly Father hid us in Christ and seated us in His heavenly domain! You have been carefully and lovingly placed here for this very moment in time. Therefore there is nothing accidental about any aspect of you. Not your birth, your family, your location, your talents, your strengths, or even your weaknesses. You were skillfully formed and marvelously made for now!

Just as we do not live by the haphazard patterns of this broken earth, we do not war according to this world's corrupted system. We have been entrusted with the ancient and incorruptible strategies and weaponry of heaven.

It is for this reason that I am honored and beyond thrilled that you have chosen to delve a bit deeper and go the extra mile to further arm yourself and increase your expertise with swords. This *Girls with Swords Fencing Manual* is meant to be used in concert with the book *Girls with Swords*. In addition to the book, you will find the corresponding DVD and CD curriculum to be an excellent complimentary resource.

The goal of this manual is to further engage you in the use of some of the invisible and invincible weapons that have been entrusted to us. I want the sword of God's Word to be fluently spoken so you become a weapon in His hand. For this to happen, the Word must first become alive within the recesses of our hearts. What lives in our hearts becomes evident in our words, and the evidence of our words become tangible in our futures.

Fencing is an art best learned in the company of others. I hope you have the opportunity to do this study as part of a gathering of like-minded sisters in arms. If you are doing this as an individual study, the Holy Spirit will act as a sparring partner to reveal both your strengths and areas of vulnerability. Whether you are part of a group or approaching this from a place of solitude, it is my truest prayer that the Spirit will be your personal trainer as my words walk you through the courses of this manual. I believe you have awakened to the reality of battle and are now ready to stand armed and unafraid. En garde!

1 | Let us begin by writing down your hopes, expectations, and possible fears for this study. (After all, you are preparing to handle a weapon.)

> · Closer to God
> · become a STRONG & CONFIDENT warrior
>
> Fears:
> Lack of understanding & distraction

Each of us will begin at varied age, life experience, and word awareness skill levels. These pages and practices will mean different things in our different seasons of life.

> *"Christianity is a battle, not a dream."*
> —Wendell Phillips

2 | How do you feel about this quote?

> Moved! Christianity has ↑ and ↓,
> you have to work for it, not just
> think "oh that would be nice."
>
> People think being a Christian is easy,
> little do they know we are TARGETED!

3 | Do you see evidence of this battle in your everyday world? Describe something you saw or heard recently:

Yes, the Islamic terrorist. Stabbing people who were not Muslim.
Faith based Killings?
OK to be gay / but not OK to PRAY in Schools!

"We do not live by the violence of a sword, but the time has come to live by the power of one."

[Page 3]

Reading of the Word

doing what Bible says   Believing   Fear?

G 4 | What do you feel the difference is between the "violence of a sword" and the "power of one"? *Acting   READING*

Violence = acting / reacting quickly not thinking it through
Actions speak louder than words?
Doing whats right

a | What is the power we live by?

The heavenly FATHERS word.
Peer pressure & Status — 20th century

The Word of God is more than a sword; it is Jesus Christ. Ultimately it is "in Christ" that we find our source of life.

And the Word became flesh and dwelt among us, and we have seen his glory, glory as of the only Son from the Father, full of grace and truth.
John 1:14

The sexual enslavement of women takes various forms: forced marriage, sexual servitude, and sex trafficking.[1]

He is our eternal Lord, Savior, living wisdom, daily bread, anchor of hope, and light on our path, just as surely as He is a high tower and a rock. Likewise we read the Word in order that it would be fleshed out in our lives so that all may know Him. It is never that we lay any of these assignments of the Word aside. But knowing there is a multitude of captive women, coupled with the realization that we are literally women targeted by the enemy, it is high time we add swords to our (Word of God) armory.

> **As you move through this fencing manual ask yourself, what God-plan does the enemy want you to miscarry?**

A Target Is Born

When Jesus was first presented for His dedication in the temple, His parents discovered He had been targeted.

And Simeon blessed them and said to Mary his mother, "Behold, this child is appointed for the fall and rising of many in Israel, and for a sign that is opposed (and a sword will pierce through your own soul also), so that thoughts from many hearts may be revealed."

Luke 2:34-35

Gendercide

- Every year, at least 2 million girls worldwide disappear because of gender discrimination.[2]
- As of 2010, the UN estimated that 117 million women are missing worldwide, most of them from China and India.[3]
- Even if male to female birth ratios were to normalize everywhere in the coming decades, the world population is likely to remain predominantly masculine until 2080.[4]
- Women in India have been assassinated, burned to death, hanged, and otherwise murdered simply for giving birth to girls.[5]

Likewise how we carry our crosses and live our lives will be a sign that causes the rise or fall of others. As we travel through these pages, don't be afraid to allow the same sword you hold in your hand to pierce your heart.

In order to bring minimum offense and greater portions of faith, hope, and love to others, we allow what we steward to first do its work on us. Throughout this study, I want you to see the sword of God's Word and the cross of Christ as instruments of war that fight in order for this world to experience God's love.

5 | Before you realized you were a target, did you already feel like a victim?

6 | Have you been able to change your vantage from that of a victim *of* the enemy's schemes to that of a threat *to* his schemes?

DAy by day.
Through prAy &
GIVING thanks

Fencing Master

You can discover what your enemy fears most by observing the means he uses to frighten you.[6]

—Eric Hoffer, American writer

7 | What areas of your life do you feel the ~~enemy has targeted?~~

(MY)
Confidence, judgement, weaknesses
↖ not trusting myself

a | Why would he target your family?

It easy to strAy from God when things are not going as planned.
When SATAN "HARMS" those that we love.

b | Your friends?

Army = close friends upport System. Make you feel alone & Different.

> *"You are a target.*
> *You might be a hero.*
> *I say "might be" because*
> *the choice is ultimately*
> *yours.*
>
> *Lisa Bevere*
> *Girls With Swords*

c | The daughters of your country?

Weakening our army, make us question GODS PLAN

8 | In what ways do you identify with Sarah Connor?

I'm just an average white girl. Nothing more nothing less
Why am I special or so Different.
WHY ME!

9 | Are you waiting for your life to begin?

Yes & no. Waiting for God to guide me

10 | Were you caught off guard and unaware?

Yes, what is my plan, How do I fit into the bigger picture.

You've been targeted. Now what's your target?

(G) 11 | You now know that everything God created women to stand for (virtue, skill, nurture, intuition, life giving, and wisdom) is under attack. How will this change your future approach to life?

I want to learn to use God's Word (sword) to strengthen the characteristics that God purposed for women. I will be more aware that these characteristics are being attacked

12 | How is the enemy currently attempting to distract you?

Not trust God's plan for me. Trying to force my OWN future.

13 | Why might the enemy want you distracted?

To turn me away from God. To want more to be FLESHY. To strip me of the characteristics God gave Me!

"The attacks on your life have much more to do with who you might be in the future than who you have been in the past."

[Page 7]

14 | How did this statement affect you? Did it bring clarity or scare you?

Clarity. God's plan is much bigger than we can understand. The circumstances now are preparing the current me, for the future me!

China has 118 males for every 100 females.[7] India has 109.[8] Pakistan has 111.[9]

15 | What might the enemy be trying to prevent or compromise in your future?

My relationship with God, Family, friends, finances.

16 | What does the word *Christ* mean?

Love - unconditional

17 | Define what it means to be anointed:

Cleansed & HEALED, from broken to blessed.

a | How do we become anointed?

We bring in the Holy Spirit

b | Why does God anoint us?

To give us power

Signify's God blessing or call on a person's life

> ⚔ *Fencing Master*
>
> The world is a dangerous place, not because of those who do bad things, but because of those who look on and do nothing.[10]
>
> —Albert Einstein

18 | In your own words, describe what your life would look like if you were alive with purpose:

I would be more loving and giving, less fleshy and trying to compare myself and things to others

✤ ✤ ✤

19 | Whose battle is this?

My battle, God's battle, Satan's battle

a | What does being a sword in His hand look like?

Using the bible's words to live by. Listening to what God's word says and obeying it.

If the enemy fails to distract you, he will oppress you in an attempt to diminish God's assignment on your life. If this tactic fails, he will sow division because what he divides he can ultimately destroy. In order to locate his strategy, assign the words *distract, diminish, divide,* or *destroy* to the following areas of your life (circle all that apply):

distract + divide

Family/marriage

Friendships *diminish*

School

Career/work relations

divide Finances/debt *distract*

Church - *divide*

Health:

Physical *diminish*

Mental *distract*

Spiritual *divide*

Community *divide*

I will put enmity between you and the woman, and between your offspring and her offspring; he shall bruise your head, and you shall bruise his heel.

Genesis 3:15

20 | Whose side does this place the woman on? God's or the serpent's?

Serpents

a | Do you believe this to be a curse, a declaration, or a bit of both?

Both, if Satan can divide man and women he can demish the bond they have with God

21 | In addition to gendercide and sex trafficking, list some other current, subtler attacks against women: (E.g., pornography).

Revealing clothing, TV & magazines, celebrities, bulling, peer pressure

On one side a relentlessly cruel enemy is perpetually bent on your destruction, and on the other side a magnificent prince of unfailing love is equally determined that you realize all he created you to be. Jesus, our Prince of Heaven, will always love you. His love is as never ending as the enmity of your assassin. The role you choose to play in this altercation is what is in question. Will you be an unarmed civilian, victim, prisoner of war, or hero?

22 | Choose today: what will it be?

Hero, God did not create me to be a victim in this (my) story

We love to watch movies and read tales of epic adventure. Don't be surprised that you have found yourself in the middle of one.

"All is summed up in the prayer which a young female human is said to have uttered recently: 'O God make me a normal twentieth-century girl!' Thanks to our labors this will mean increasingly: 'Make me a minx, a moron and a parasite.'"[11]

C.S. Lewis, *The Screwtape Letters*

23 | Before reading this quote, were you hoping for normal?

Yes

(G) 24 | How would you describe the normal or typical twenty-first century girl? In addition to words, feel free to include pictures.

Skinny, perfect hair, lots of girl friends, popular, high heels, well dressed. Clean, wears make up

a | Which pop stars are typical?

Jennifer Aniston
Beyonce

b | Which are atypical?

Jo - Fixer Upper

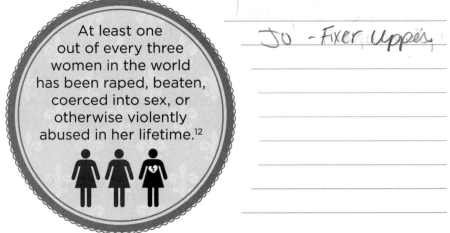

At least one out of every three women in the world has been raped, beaten, coerced into sex, or otherwise violently abused in her lifetime.[12]

(G) 25 | What is the focus or motivation behind your prayers?

50 % me 50 % God in I want to be a more giving woman, helping others

a | What percentage of your prayers are reactionary or need-based?
(For example: *This is happening, or I need help, so I pray.*)

60 %

b | How often are your prayers crafted from the Scriptures?

10 %

Let's review the prayer Jesus modeled:

*"Pray then like this: 'Our Father in heaven, hallowed be your name.
Your kingdom come, your will be done, on earth as it is in heaven.
Give us this day our daily bread, and forgive us our debts, as we also
have forgiven our debtors. And lead us not into temptation, but deliver
us from evil.' For if you forgive others their trespasses, your heavenly
Father will also forgive you, but if you do not forgive others
their trespasses, neither will your Father forgive your trespasses."*
Matthew 6:9-15

26 | Is this prayer still relevant? Is it limited or in any way less powerful in
today's culture?

Yes

a | What is the substance behind this prayer?

Treat others as God would treat them. Ask for forgiveness

27 | How can you partner with heaven to structure your prayers?

Use God's word, be thankful, don't demand. Be patient, ask if its God's Will.

The Creator of heaven and earth is the Architect and Author of our lives. **It is time for the daughters of this twenty-first century to echo heaven's words.** Perhaps the longing within you is larger than your words may yet know how to form, and thus the very reason you need a sword.

I believe in one way or another you long to be an extraordinary, heroic daughter of the eternal Most High God—one who behaves virtuously, matures brilliantly, and lives with the intent of enhancing the lives of others.

One of the purposes of this book is to help you construct the type of bold, faith-filled prayers (swords) that will specifically address your moment in history. Pray the following scriptures out loud over your life:

Sword Words

Not that I have already obtained this or am already perfect, but I press on to make it my own, because Christ Jesus has made me his own.
Philippians 3:12

I press on toward the goal for the prize of the upward call of God in Christ Jesus.
Philippians 3:14

I can do all things through him who strengthens me.
Philippians 4:13

Is there one scripture that particularly resonated with you? If so, highlight it here or in your Bible.

Becoming who God created you to be is at once best offense and defense against all the enemy's strategy.

28 | Do you believe this?

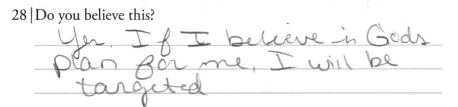

Yes. If I believe in Gods plan for me, I will be targeted

We create an environment for this to happen when we say what He says about us.

29 | Given this insight, and drawing upon the inspiration of the scriptures and endearments God has whispered into your life, write His description of you: (Feel free to add onto this as it grows within you.)

But the more they were oppressed, the more they multiplied and the more they spread abroad. And the Egyptians were in dread of the people of Israel.
Exodus 1:12

30 | God can multiply us in the very areas where the enemy seeks to oppress us. God will often use the very forces that are meant to contain and divide to release and unite. Is there evidence of this response among women?

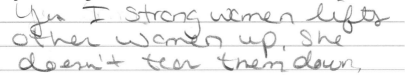

Yes. I strong women lifts other women up, she doesn't tear them down,

31 | Did you know the cruelty of bullies and oppressors was driven by their own fear?

Yes.

a | Give a local example of this (at school, work, etcetera):

Bullied in schools, oppressed homes or sexual abuse

G 32 | Just as Pharaoh hoped to stop an army from amassing, and Herod hoped to stop a king from ascending through the targeted murder of the males, what has been foretold that Satan hopes to stop through his onslaught against the daughters?

Sword Play

From any of the media sources available to you, share one example of this gendercide.

Room for Reflection

Gendercide = early abortion? more in secret, modern day looks down upon gendercide

Fencing Lessons

- ✠ You are a target—you can choose to be a hero.
- ✠ We are often attacked in areas of future strength.
- ✠ This could be more about your future than about your past.
- ✠ The enemy attacks what he feels threatened by.
- ✠ He uses tactics of distraction, demeaning, division, and destruction.

SKILL CHECK
You are a target because this world needs our hero—Jesus.

En Garde

Here I am, ready to be alive with purpose.

Impressions

(1) Andrea Parrot and Nina Cummings, *Sexual Enslavement of Girls and Women Worldwide* (Westport, CT: Praeger Publishers, 2008), 13. (2) Nicholas D. Kristof and Sheryl WuDunn, *Half the Sky: Turning Oppression into Opportunity for Women Worldwide* (New York: Alfred A. Knopf, 2009), xv. (3) UNFPA, *Sex Imbalances at Birth: Current trends, consequences and policy implications* (Bangkok, Thailand: UNFPA Asia and the Pacific Regional Office, 2012), 2, accessed January 29, 2013, http://www.unfpa.org/public/home/publications/pid/12405. (4) Ibid, p. 48 (5) "Killed for having a girl," The 50 Million Missing Campaign, accessed February 18, 2013, http://violenceonindianwomen.wordpress.com/tag/killed-for-having-a-girl/. (6) "Eric Hoffer quotes," ThinkExist.com, accessed January 29, 2013, http://thinkexist.com/quotation/you_can_discover_what_your_enemy_fears_most_by/10727.html. (7) Human Rights Watch, *World Report 2012: Events of 2011* (Human Rights Watch, 2012), 323, accessed January 29, 2013, http://www.hrw.org/world-report-2012. (8) See note 3., p. 20. (9) See note 2. (10) Albert Einstein quote, "QuotingQuotes.com," accessed March 12, 2013, http://quotingquotes.com/14563/. (11) C.S. Lewis, *The Screwtape Letters* (New York: HarperCollins, 1942), 200. (12) "Gender Based Violence," International Justice Mission, accessed January 29, 2013, http://ijm.org/resources.

2

A Sword Is Born

*And each man stands with his face in the light
of his own drawn sword, ready to do what a hero can.*
Elizabeth Barrett Browning

I love this quote. We fight with faces alight. We do not wear clouded, angry countenances, for we are daughters of light. The sword we bear is our own; it is the one that fits in our hands. It is the Word of God that we have practiced and found true. Our sword is not an accessory. It is drawn, and we are ever ready. It is quite possible that the creation of swords predates our own.

> *He drove out the man, and at the east of the garden of Eden
> he placed the cherubim and a flaming sword that turned
> every way to guard the way to the tree of life.*
> Genesis 3:24

When I read this description of a flaming sword that rotated, I realized suddenly that our earthbound sabers of metal are cold and lifeless. The guardian sword carried by an angel in Genesis moved on its own; even so, it is no match for the sword that levels nations:

*From his [Jesus] mouth comes a sharp sword with which to strike down
the nations, and he will rule them with a rod of iron. He will tread
the winepress of the fury of the wrath of God the Almighty.*
Revelation 19:15

It is interesting to note that this sword is spoken. The Message version
says it this way:

*The One with the sharp-biting sword draws from the sheath
of his mouth—out come the sword words...*
Revelation 2:12

We also know from Proverbs:

*Death and life are in the power of the tongue,
and those who love it will eat its fruits.*
Proverbs 18:21

There is no doubt that our human words can release blessings or curses,
life or death. This is the very reason we need the Word of God, that we
may learn how to master our own words.

GOD'S WORD is a GOD SWORD

If God hid a sword in His Word, it would appear He did not want this
point lost on us!

Sword Words

*And take the helmet of salvation, and the sword of the Spirit,
which is the word of God.*
Ephesians 6:17

Think with me for a moment. When Paul wrote Ephesians, believers did
not have individual Bibles that they carried with them. There were letters to the churches, but for the most part they carried the Word through
speech. They had to speak the Word. Nowadays we do not "need" to speak

the Word because we read what we can so easily carry. "Out loud" is almost unheard of. Too often we do not wear our sword, let alone draw it. Instead the sword is on our bedside tables, bookshelves, or perhaps our laptops or phones.

When I received my first Bible, John encouraged me to read it **out loud** as often as possible. Looking back, this may very well have saved my life. Reading out loud to yourself engages you on multiple levels: you read (*see*) and *hear* as you *speak*. It slows you down a bit, but at the same time it causes you to process the Word through multiple channels of your brain all at once. Brain scientists are now saying what God encouraged us to do so long ago: declare His wonders from one generation to another!

> Twenty-three percent of young Christians who disconnected from the Church said they left because "the Bible is not taught clearly or often enough."[1]

Yet have we become so familiar with God's Word (because it is so readily available) that it is rarely read as a sword? Don't get me wrong; it is used as an instrument of study and devotion, but rarely as a weapon.

"I had an overwhelming sense that far too many of God's daughters in this generation are unarmed. Not only would this mean they are ill equipped and unprepared. It would also mean they are at risk and incredibly vulnerable to deception. In the last days our enemy will intensify his assaults with the double-edged sword of false teachers and brethren coupled with self-deception."

[Page 19]

In light of this insight, I want to share this dream a young girl passed onto me:

> *About a year ago, God gave me a dream. It was a battle, and for the most part, I just saw girls and women on the battlefield. There was a war going on. The opposition was firing off guns and bombs, and for some reason the girls on the battlefield only had swords. At first not*

every girl had a sword; I didn't and the friends I saw didn't. Mostly we would be praying, and the ground literally shifted every few minutes. Then my view changed and I was watching myself. I was wearing army camouflage. All of a sudden I was holding a sword that was pointed down. I shoved it into the ground and the ground shifted again.

Ever since that dream, God has really been speaking to me about putting on the armor of God and preparing for a battle without common weapons (like guns). The girls and women of today are heading into a battle but are being surrounded in prayer by a fellowship of believers. I believe this book is something God will use to connect the dots for so many others, and I'm excited to see the epic army of Girls with Swords that God is preparing and molding.

1 | Share what came to mind as you read this dream.

> Finding my army of women. By surrounding myself with strong women, it encourages me to pick up my sword.

First, we cannot escape the point that she and her friends found themselves on a battlefield initially unarmed and unprepared, while the opposition was fully armed with the weapons of this realm (guns and bombs).

I found it thought-provoking that the ground shifted in response to prayer, as well as when the sword was thrust into the ground like a stake. It was as though she knew the sword (God's Word) could be used both as an anchor to ground her and as an instrument that takes ground. The earth we walk upon responds to the words of its Creator.

G) 2 | What is your church presently doing to arm its daughters?

> Preaching the TRUE word of God to the Father's daughters

Such women are forever following new teachings,
but they are never able to understand the truth.
2 Timothy 3:7, NLT

When I read this verse from 2 Timothy, I have to wonder if these women were never able to come into the knowledge of the truth because they were hearers of it only:

But be doers of the word, and not hearers only, deceiving yourselves.
James 1:22

Whenever we fail to apply what we have learned, we open ourselves up to an environment of deception. When women (or men) fail to apply what they learn, their lives become journeys to "the next." They are always onto the next new teaching, next husband, next wife, next friend, next church, or next job. These "nexts" keep them from remembering the last teaching they have yet to live. It has been my experience that God has me circle around truth until it encircles me by dropping from my head to my heart. Some of the "doing" of the Word is not fun. Some lessons I'd prefer to skip, but if we want to come into truth, we can't. Often I've wondered if the Church has inadvertently fostered some of this by encouraging study of truths over the practice of them. This seems to be a significant pattern for women.

FENCING FACT
The sword is known as the "queen of weapons."[2]

If we know, we must do. Since the objective of this book is to arm you for battle, at the end of the day, you must lay hold of truth with both hands. Like the daughter in the dream, you must hold your ground as you arm others.

3 | Write a few ways you can get involved with this aim of making the sword of God's Word a reality in your life. (These could range from the practice of prayer or serving your community to loving your husband—anything that means intentionally doing the Word.)

I need to practice prayer
by using God's word in
thankfulness

In times of battle, swords should be put to use. One of the ways this happens is by bringing the sword of God's Word into the reality of our lives.

"The knowledge of what is good without practicing it, turns frequently to evil."
—C. Martelli, fencing master (1819)

Isn't it fascinating that this fencing principle so closely parallels the scripture in James? In Martelli's era, fencing was more than a sport: it was intertwined with nobility and chivalry as a way of life. Likewise, in our lives, we cannot separate the practice of what is good from the Word.

Reforge the Sword

You may have found it surprising that God would speak to me using a phrase from a movie scene I barely remembered. I have learned that God will speak to us in any way possible. Too often we complicate what is meant to be natural. There is nothing unusual about a father speaking to his children at any time and through any means possible. Regardless of the means, His words will *never* contradict His Word.

"I heard the Spirit whisper that far too many factions of Christ's body wield only pieces and fragments of his Word and no longer lift his Word as a whole. The Spirit also said that hardships (economic, natural, governmental, cultural, and social) will be coming upon the earth with increased frequency and force. These trials will ultimately serve to unite his people with cause and purpose. And as God's Word is lifted high in all its weight and authority, answers to these ensuing issues will be revealed....
Joined together, all these parts were mighty and useful and clearly represented a sword's function and proper use. Isolated, they were edges without points, metal without power, and blades without momentum."

[Page 22-23]

4 | Do you believe this is the state we are in?

_____

_____

5 | Do you see the fragmented and the fractional lifted over our lives rather than the whole?

_____

_____

6 | Do you believe a declaration of whole truth has the power to alter this?

_____

_____

Fencing Master

Truth will ultimately prevail where there is pains to bring it to light.[3]

—George Washington

a | What is a life-altering God-truth you presently feel challenged to embrace?

_____

_____

_____

_____

Hard truths make us one. The cross ultimately unifies. The enemy authors division. He laughs as we foolishly wield our divided words—or words that divide—when ultimately their power is in their whole.

7 | What is a practical way you can be an agent of unity today?

_____

_____

_____

_____

Recently in a conference call about the *Girls with Swords* book launch, I realized just how hesitant women are to declare God's Word with authority. For some, the reason was that they don't know the Word; others didn't know they could declare it. The Word of God is alive, powerful, perfect, and pure. Why should any of us be afraid to declare our Father's words? Better that we tremble to wield our own words rather than draw back from His.

Do you fight this fear?

A. I have in the past

B. I do currently

C. All of the above

In the past, I've likewise posed truth as a shadowed question rather than as His brilliant answer—simply because I was a woman. But I refuse to do so any longer. There is far too much at risk for me to falter.

"What I heard and saw was a charge to declare His Holy word in all of the wisdom of its counsel and wonder of its strength. It was an invitation to remake the human language in the image of the divine rather than strip the word of God of its divinity to make it human."
[Page 23]

Please do not imagine I am referring to a return to the King James Version (though if that is your favorite version, go for it!). It is a matter of our source. Are our words formed by merely human interaction, or are they touched by the divine?

8 | What are some of the ways the Word of God might influence your speech?

_____

_____

_____

_____

_____

Sword Words

Let no corrupting talk come out of your mouths, but only such as is good for building up, as fits the occasion, that it may give grace to those who hear.
Ephesians 4:29

There are both corrupt and incorruptible conversations happening everyday.

9 | What does incorruptible communication do for the hearers?

_____

_____

_____

_____

_____

"…From the ashes a fire shall be woken.
A light from the shadow shall spring.
Renewed shall be blade that was broken.
The crownless again shall be king.…
Reforge the sword."
—*The Return of the King*

Can I be brutally honest? The season in which I wrote this book felt like a pile of ashes—yet those ashes woke a fire. As I found my quickening, light burst upon my shadow and I looked into the Word of God with new eyes. I was not queen—let alone king—but in that season my King's Word became my standard. The Word of God is not black and red ink on fragile tissue pages; it is fire and steel for our souls!

Sparring

Ⓖ If you believe this, answer the following *discussion questions* frankly:

10 | Are we using the Word to mark history or make it?

11 | Do we still celebrate what was to the neglect of what might be?

> ⚔ *Fencing Master*
>
> Let us accept truth, even when it surprises us and alters our views.[4]
>
> —George Sand, female novelist

12 | Is God's Word our final authority?

13 | What might happen if we lived the Word that we've studied?

You are the daughter of a WARRIOR whose eternal creative WORD in YOUR mouth is a LIVING INVINCIBLE sword in your HAND.

Lisa Bevere · girls with swords

14 | Are we declaring or interpreting the Word?

_____

_____

_____

_____

_____

15 | Does the Church (or Christians) have a reputation for *wounding* or *healing* with the Word?

_____

_____

_____

_____

Ancient Paths

> *Thus says the LORD: "Stand by the roads, and look,*
> *and ask for the ancient paths, where the good way is;*
> *and walk in it, and find rest for your souls."*
> Jeremiah 6:16

I believe this is an invitation for us to look for paths and ways that are the ancient, meaning *eternal*, rather than the ancient as in *old*. The sword of God's Word will separate our earthly motivations and establish heaven's intent.

This is the very reason our Lord said we'd need a sword in this new season.

> *He said to them, "But now let the one who has a moneybag take it,*
> *and likewise a knapsack. And let the one who has no sword*
> *sell his cloak and buy one."*
> Luke 22:36

Sister, if there is a choice to be made, forget the coat—get a sword! Read the following passage from Matthew:

And behold, one of those who were with Jesus stretched out his hand and drew his sword and struck the servant of the high priest and cut off his ear. Then Jesus said to him, "Put your sword back into its place. For all who take the sword will perish by the sword. Do you think that I cannot appeal to my Father, and he will at once send me more than twelve legions of angels? But how then should the Scriptures be fulfilled, that it must be so?"
Matthew 26:51-54

Anyone else with Peter on this, or is it only me? Here is the best way I can break this down: the right thing at the wrong time becomes the wrong thing! You don't stop your Lord from being taken when He has told you repeatedly and clearly that the cross is a must for the Scriptures to be fulfilled. The hour had come.

But I have said these things to you, that when their hour comes you may remember that I told them to you. I did not say these things to you from the beginning, because I was with you.
John 16:4

We are not on the eve of the cross and frightened in a garden. We are not hiding while our Lord's body is cold in a grave. We are armed for His return. We are daughters of the coming day foretold by Isaiah.

I have created the blacksmith who fans the coals beneath the forge and makes the weapons of destruction. And I have created the armies that destroy.
But in that coming day *no weapon turned against you will succeed. You will silence every voice raised up to accuse you. These benefits are enjoyed by the servants of the Lord; their vindication will come from me. I, the Lord, have spoken!*
Isaiah 54:16-17, NLT

Our God turns death into life and weakness into strength. Our God calls the end a new beginning and vindication a benefit! It is time to see the fire springing to life and the sword reborn.

This dynamic alone helps us understand why, at times, Jesus appeared to contradict Himself. When we try to understand eternal perspective from an earthbound mindset, it is easy to err. This is why I believe with all my heart that Jesus did not mean for us to wield visible swords but invisible ones.

> *Do not think that I have come to bring peace to the earth.*
> *I have not come to bring peace, but a sword.*
> Matthew 10:34

This verse is followed by a description of all the degrees of separation that will occur when the sword of God's Word overtakes one's life. It is not a metal sword; it is the very sword that separates soul from spirit. Jesus goes on to say:

> *And whoever does not take his cross and follow me is not worthy of me.*
> *Whoever finds his life will lose it, and whoever loses his life*
> *for my sake will find it.*
> Matthew 10:38-39

16 | What areas of your life might this sword want to separate?

_____

_____

_____

_____

_____

Fencing Master

The truth is more important than the facts.[5]

—Frank Lloyd Wright

a | What is it you hope to find in return?

_____

_____

_____

_____

_____

_____

17 | The sword of God's Word has the power to reveal motives and join or separate relationships, scattering some in terror or uniting us as one body in courage.

a | List two scriptures that divide:

_____

_____

_____

_____

_____

_____

_____

b | List two scriptures that unite:

_____

_____

_____

_____

_____

_____

"The sword is truth."

In the history of fencing, it was believed that the one who won the duel was the one who was truthful and honorable. We know now the victory went to the one who had mastered the art of fencing. Here is our chance to see the sword be truth, not in a duel to the death but through a fight for life.

Fencing: The terms *sword fighting* and *fencing* can be used interchangeably. Fencing is derived from the word *defense*; we have no greater defense than the Word of God.

Prayer

Heavenly Father,

I ask that Your sword would impart courage as it separates me from anything and anyone that keep me from You. As I declare Your eternal Word, teach me Your ancient ways. Light any shadowed areas of my life with Your truth. Reforge the sword until it is more alive in my life than a metal saber would feel in my hand. Jesus, show me what I need to lay aside to buy my sword.

Sword Play

This week, ask God to reveal a challenge or opportunity in which you can wield a truth previously learned from your study of the Word. When you gather again, share what happened with your fellow sword sisters.

Room for Reflection

_____

_____

_____

_____

Fencing Lessons

- ⚜ God's Word is a God sword.
- ⚜ This sword must be put to use on the field of battle.
- ⚜ Be a doer of the Word.
- ⚜ The enemy is not threatened by a fragment of a weapon.
- ⚜ When swords appear, motives are revealed.

SKILL CHECK

Fencing is one of the few sports where being a male holds little advantage. Sister, hone your intuitive awareness and increase your sensitivity to His Spirit and authority in prayer.

En Garde

I will declare the Word of God with boldness and without question because it is my Father's will. The Word is alive, pure, and perfect!

Impressions

(1) "Six Reasons Young Christians Leave Church," The Barna Group, accessed January 31, 2013, http://www.barna.org/teens-next-gen-articles/528-six-reasons-young-christians-leave-church. (2) Nick Evangelista, *The Art and Science of Fencing* (Lincolnwood, IL: Masters Press, 1996), 7. (3) "George Washington," BrainyQuote.com, accessed February 1, 2013, http://www.brainyquote.com/quotes/quotes/g/george-wash384189.html. (4) "Truth," WomensQuotes.com, accessed February 1, 2013, http://womensquotes.com/truth/truth. (5) "Frank Lloyd Wright," BrainyQuote.com, accessed February 1, 2013, http://www.brainyquote.com/quotes/quotes/f/franklloyd103784.html.

You Might Be a Hero

*We can be in our day what the heroes of faith were
in their day—but remember at the time
they didn't know they were heroes.*

—A. W. Tozer

It would seem the present can distort our reality and that the passage of time alone has the power to reveal. I've always assumed the heroes of the faith knew they were heroes. But more than likely, they just felt like outcasts that the sword of God's Word had separated for His purposes. In most of the action movies we watch, there is a brilliant, highly skilled "someone" who is already capable of doing the extraordinary and who decides to use their power for good. Not so with us. More often than not we begin like a Sarah (both Sarah Connor and Sarah, our mother of faith), protesting...

I haven't fought a battle.

I haven't borne a child.

I haven't any money.

I'm single.

I'm married.

I'm old.

I'm young.

I haven't done anything.

None of these matter. You *will* do something, because God has a plan for you. He is just waiting for you to give Him permission to insert you into His plan and scrap your own. It all begins with our willingness and ends with us extraordinarily empowered.

⚔ *Fencing Master*

It takes courage to grow up and turn out to be who you really are.[1]

—E.E. Cummings

God Makes Heroes Out of Nobodies

We enter into this story by faith. There are no try-outs; if you are ready, you're in. God has already written you into the storyline of faith heroes, and it is an epic of triumphant proportions filled with miracles, battles, signs, and wonders.

> *But the story we're given is a God-story, not an Abraham-story.*
> Romans 4:2, The Message

This is not my story or your story; it is His story. When God is looking to do something grander than we can design, He brings us into His plans—rather than blessing what we have constructed.

> *For what does the Scripture say? "Abraham believed God,*
> *and it was counted to him as righteousness."*
> Romans 4:3

And in The Message,

> *"Abraham entered into what God was doing for him, and*
> *that was the turning point. He trusted God to set him right*
> *instead of trying to be right on his own."*
> Romans 4:3

1 | Are you ready to do the same? In your own words, write out your permission for God to make a somebody out of a nobody and to make something out of the empty areas of your life:

_____

_____

_____

_____

_____

_____

_____

This action shows that you believe that "in Him" we are more than conquerors. *In Him* our perspective changes and we are granted authority. Likewise the greatest hero ever, Jesus, worked with His Father:

> *So Jesus said to them, "Truly, truly, I say to you, **the Son can do nothing of his own accord**, but only what he sees the Father doing. For whatever the Father does, that the Son does likewise."*
> John 5:19

Accord means "in agreement, unity," and "in harmony with." Jesus, the only begotten Son of God, did nothing out of sync with His Father. Likewise we, His hero daughters, accomplish nothing of eternal value if we don't likewise follow His lead!

There is risk involved here. It can be scary to believe and say what we have yet to see.

> *We call Abraham "father" not because he got God's attention by living like a saint, but because **God made something out of Abraham when he was a nobody**. Isn't that what we've always read in Scripture, God saying to Abraham, "I set you up as father of many peoples"? Abraham was first named "father" and then became a father because he dared to trust God to do what only God could do: raise the dead to life, **with a word make something out of nothing**.*
> Romans 4:17, The Message

2 | Our heavenly Father specializes in the impossible and the improbable. God called Abraham "father of many" long before he became one. What is it that God calls you that you are yet trying to be or achieve in your own strength?

_____

_____

_____

_____

Holy? Strong? Fearless?

a | If you struggle with any of these, record a scripture that bears the power to *with a word make something out of nothing* in the space below.

_____

_____

_____

That "something" very well may be to form a courageous action hero out of a formerly complacent, broken daughter. When we enter into God's actions on our behalf, we become action heroes. Our ancestors distinguished themselves from the masses by their *acts of faith* or *faith actions*. They attained the status of heroic men and women in the history of God.

When we enter into God's actions on our behalf, we become action heroes.

Heroes Are People of Substance

Now faith is the substance of things hoped for,
the evidence of things not seen.
Hebrews 11:1 KJV

Daughters of faith are daughters of substance.

3 | Define *substance*:

_____

_____

_____

_____

(G) 4 | Read Hebrews 11 and let your heart soar. Without filtering it by what you have seen or experienced, what did this passage awaken in you?

_____

_____

_____

_____

> **Fencing Master**
>
> There is a certain enthusiasm in liberty that makes human nature rise above itself, in acts of bravery and heroism.
>
> —Alexander Hamilton

It's time we joined their ranks by adding action to faith! Those who believe take action.

> *So also faith by itself, if it does not have works, is dead.*
> James 2:17

This is as silly as believing to get pregnant while refusing to have sex with your husband. Just as babies are conceived through an act of love, faith is given substance through an action of faith. A faith action could be something as small as reaching out with a word of kindness or as large as leaving behind all you've known. *Believe* means *do*. As we declare the Word, we let it have its way and do it. Being in Christ means we are graced to do.

> *Do you want to be shown, you foolish person, that faith apart from works is useless? Was not Abraham our father justified by works when he offered up his son Isaac on the altar? You see that faith was active along with his works, and faith was completed by his works.*
> James 2:20-22

5 | Review the list of faith actions on pages 38-39 of *Girls with Swords*. Choose one that you can attach action to. Write both the listed "act" and your personal action in the space below.

_____

_____

_____

_____

Heroes Have Attitude

You have probably heard that "your attitude determines your altitude." We all know people with serious attitude. I'm not addressing an attitude that distinguishes you among people. I want you to bear an attitude of heaven. This happens as we read, believe, declare, and live God's Word. We adopt heaven's perspective, refuse to live by the limits of this earth, and enter into God's limitless kingdom.

Our broken lives are healed, and we reach out to heal others. As descendants of faith, this is our heritage: we can face peril in the same manner that we embrace wonders.

The heroes of faith went before us and braved hardships such as: torture, abuse (not by their spouses), whips, dungeons and chains, stoning, and murder. Some were blessed, while others wandered around in animal skins—homeless, friendless, and **powerless in their day**.

> ### *Fencing Master*
> When you have resolved to be great, abide by yourself, and do not try to reconcile yourself with the world. The heroic cannot be common, nor the common heroic.[3]
>
> —Ralph Waldo Emerson

I want to jump on that point once again. You may think you are powerless when in fact, you are not! There are many authors who had very little influence in their day but who have a great deal of influence in our day. Jesus had very little influence in His hometown in His day, yet He would travel to neighboring cities and see signs, wonders, and miracles. While Jeremiah was in a pit, he never imagined we would be reading his words. "In their day" was not the end of their stories—any more than it is the end of yours!

This earth is not our home. Isn't it time we lived and acted like citizens of heaven rather than hoping this broken world will acknowledge our deeds? Our day is coming. These heroes may have felt powerless in their day, but they are powerful in ours. The Bible describes them as those "of whom the world was not worthy—wandering about in deserts and mountains, and in dens and caves of the earth" (Hebrews 11:38).

6 | Do you want to live in a way that makes you more a citizen of heaven than earth?

_____

_____

_____

Don't look around: look ahead!

Heroes Seize Their Moment

*[They] **quenched the power of fire,** escaped the edge of the sword,*
were made strong out of weakness, became mighty in war,
put foreign armies to flight.
Hebrews 11:34

When I read the account of my interaction with the Waldo Canyon Fire, it is borderline embarrassing! I was a "she of little faith," so busy writing and studying that I almost missed a chance to be part of an act of faith. I was weary in writing and negligent of my part of well-doing.

When your prayers seem to have gone unanswered, you may begin to question God's will. In Ephesians we learn that rather than questioning and backing down, we are to stand firm.

Therefore take up the whole armor of God, that you may be able to
withstand in the evil day, and having done all, to stand firm.
Ephesians 6:13

So many battles you win by remaining constant. If you are faltering, call a friend like we did. Call someone who is not surrounded by smoke. Call someone who is an action hero; they will sharpen your resolve and dare you to only believe. God knew there would be times we needed these types of friends.

> *Again I say to you, if two of you agree on earth about anything they ask,*
> *it will be done for them by my Father in heaven. For where two or*
> *three are gathered in my name, there am I among them.*
> Matthew 18:19-20

7 | Who is it that you can call?

_____

_____

_____

8 | Have you learned something that will benefit you in a future battle? Write down a stone of remembrance here:

_____

_____

_____

_____

Heroes Are Part of a Connected Legacy

> *Each one of these people of faith died not*
> *yet having in hand what was promised,*
> *but still believing. How did they do it?*
> *They saw it way off in the distance, waved*
> *their greeting, and accepted the fact that*
> *they were transients in this world.*
> Hebrews 11:13, The Message

Fencing Master

The hero draws inspiration from the virtue of his ancestors.[4]

—Johann von Goethe

I believe we are part of the company they saw in the distance. Sometimes I can barely grasp the wonder of it all. These legends chose to look to the future and to the One they had placed all their hope and faith upon.

And all these, though commended through their faith, did not receive
what was promised, since God had provided something better for us,
that apart from us they should not be made perfect.
Hebrews 11:39-40

9 | Did you realize you had been linked to the promises that had been
made to them?

How epic: we are part of the final act of this story. All of their heroic acts
are waiting to be completed when they are joined together with ours.

(G) 10 | How does this make you feel?

> ✠ They wandered in harsh conditions; we gather in
> air-conditioned buildings.
> ✠ They were homeless; we have found our home in the
> house of God.
> ✠ They sang alone in the wilderness; we lift our voices
> among thousands.
> ✠ They were hands off; God asks us to be hands on.

11 | What is the faith substance we contribute to this legacy of faith, then
and now? After reading these comparisons, what are your thoughts?

The following verses lend us the reason (or the *therefore*) behind our race:

*Therefore, since we are surrounded by so great a cloud
of witnesses, let us also lay aside every weight,
and sin which clings so closely, and let us run with
endurance the race that is set before us, looking to
Jesus, the founder and perfecter of our faith,
who for the joy that was set before him endured
the cross, despising the shame, and is seated
at the right hand of the throne of God.*
Hebrews 12:1-2

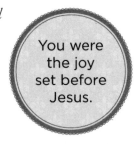

12| Do you believe these heroes of old are the ones cheering us on?

_____

_____

_____

_____

As this realization—that *in Him* we are "heroes," and that He is the hero within us—grows, any fear you initially felt when you learned you were a target should be squelched. Being a hero is now your act of worship.

Sword Words

Throw your shoulders back and declare:
*"I am positioned for overwhelming triumph because I am
'from God and have overcome them, for he who is
in [me] is greater than he who is in the world'" (1 John 4:4).*

Heroes Are Superhuman

*The godly people in the land are my true heroes!
I take pleasure in them!*
Psalm 16:3, NLT

(G) 13 | What does it mean to be godly?

_____

_____

_____

> *Not by might, nor by power, but by my Spirit, says the LORD of hosts.*
> Zechariah 4:6

God's Spirit is described as both mighty and powerful, so the might and power that we labor in is not our own. Humans operate according to this world's motivations; we are to rise above that. Humans allow strife and jealousy to drive them; heroes are led by a higher way.

> *For while there is jealousy and strife among you, are you*
> *not of the flesh and behaving only in a human way?*
> 1 Corinthians 3:3

Because we are now daughters of God, hidden in Christ, we can behave like our Father. This means any past excuse of *I'm only human* no longer stands.

Human isn't large enough. By eliminating jealousy and strife from the equation of our lives, we choose to walk in one accord and in agreement with our Father and His purpose. We answer to our Father, not our feelings. God is our power source, and we are accountable to the One who empowers us and has granted us the privilege of sharing His name: Jesus.

Heroes Are Brave

Heroes are *always brave,* but don't imagine that *always brave* translates to *never afraid.*

14 | Can you work with this description?

_____

_____

_____

15 | You don't have to *feel* brave to be brave. You just have to *choose* to *do* what is brave—and sometimes that means only five minutes longer. Record an incident when you stood bravely "five minutes longer":

_____

_____

_____

_____

_____

_____

Reacting does not equal choosing. Fear will drive you to react, but as you become more skillful with the sword, you will choose your response with the intent of honoring your Father—rather than for protecting yourself.

FENCING FACT
To have a say in the matter, to choose your response— this is a real fencer.[5]

We have the right to choose. This is what distinguishes the base and abandoned from the loved and adopted.

Heroes Have Something More to Them

Heroes tend to champion causes, rather than champion themselves. The motivation of serving those outside themselves drives them to risk being more daring, able, compassionate, willing, responsible, and insightful. Heroes understand there is always more than what meets the eye. Heroes are not afraid to stand up or to stand out. This willingness to rise above the realm of normal makes them appear extraordinary.

Fencing Master
True heroism...is not the urge to surpass all others at whatever cost, but the urge to serve others at whatever cost.[6]

—Arthur Ashe

16 | Tough question time: when was the last time you championed something that actually didn't benefit you? Think of something that didn't add goodwill to your name—perhaps no one even knew about it.

_____

_____

_____

_____

Heroes do things because they see that they are right, not because they want to be seen. There is an unseen marking on your life. It seals in spite of your strengths and weaknesses!

God compensates for our weaknesses because His intent is that, together as one body, we would be strong.

Sword Play

Call a friend and recount a time when you saw God move through an act of faith in your lives.

Room for Reflection

_____

_____

_____

_____

_____

_____

Read Ephesians 6:10-18 out loud (page 50 of *Girls with Swords*).

There is a massive amount of information in this passage. Let's itemize the significant points, because these verses in Ephesians outline the mandate of this book.

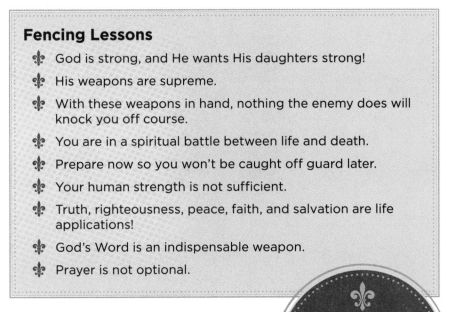

Fencing Lessons

- ✤ God is strong, and He wants His daughters strong!
- ✤ His weapons are supreme.
- ✤ With these weapons in hand, nothing the enemy does will knock you off course.
- ✤ You are in a spiritual battle between life and death.
- ✤ Prepare now so you won't be caught off guard later.
- ✤ Your human strength is not sufficient.
- ✤ Truth, righteousness, peace, faith, and salvation are life applications!
- ✤ God's Word is an indispensable weapon.
- ✤ Prayer is not optional.

It is my prayer that by the end of this study, not one of these points will remain in question!

SKILL CHECK
The process of becoming a hero is giving God permission to make something out of nothing in your life.

En Garde

As the daughters of God draw their swords, the enemy draws back.

we can be in
· OUR DAY ·
what the heroes of faith
were in their day...
⌘ BUT REMEMBER ⌘
at the time
.... they didn't know
☆ THEY were HEROES ☆
A.W. TOZER
lisa bevere · GIRLS WITH SWORDS

Impressions

(1) "E.E. Cummings quote," QuotationsBook.com, accessed February 18, 2013, http://quotationsbook.com/quote/8690. (2) "Alexander Hamilton," Wikiquote, accessed March 12, 2013, http://en.wikiquote.org/wiki/Alexander_Hamilton. (3) "Ralph Waldo Emerson," QuotationsBook.com, accessed February 18, 2013, http://quotationsbook.com/quote/18983/. (4) "Hero/Heroism quotes," Quoteland.com, accessed February 1, 2013, http://www.quoteland.com/topic/HeroesHeroism-Quotes/276/?pg=2. (5) Nick Evangelista, *The Inner Game of Fencing: Excellence in Form, Technique, Strategy, and Spirit* (Lincolnwood, IL: Masters Press, 2000). (6) "Arthur Ashe quotes," ThinkExist.com, accessed February 1, 2013, http://thinkexist.com/quotation/true_heroism_is_remarkably_sober-very_undramatic/222045.html.

4

The Battleground

We are locked in a battle.
This is not a friendly...discussion.
It is a life and death conflict between
the spiritual hosts of wickedness
and those who claim the name of Christ.
—Francis A. Schaeffer[1]

1 | Who are our real enemies?

_____

_____

_____

2 | Where do we fight?

_____

_____

_____

3 | I hope you are becoming increasingly aware that the unseen governs much of what we see. Let's test this theory.

a | Can you see your thoughts?

_____

b | Can you see your words?

_____

And yet the consequences and fruit of these two *invisible* forces are evident in our every waking day. So it is not only foolish, but also dangerous, to imagine something outside our realm of notice has no influence on us. It is time we use both our thoughts and our words to our advantage. This approach takes some training because the enemy knows the power of both. He counters by attempting to engage our minds and mouths in an ongoing wrestling match.

> *For we do not wrestle against flesh and blood, but against the rulers,*
> *against the authorities, against the cosmic powers over this present*
> *darkness, against the spiritual forces of evil in the heavenly places.*
> Ephesians 6:12

If we wrestle not with flesh and blood, then a whole lot of us have wasted a lot of energy and time wrestling someone who is not even in the ring! This means that when we face our real opponent, we are too exhausted to recognize him. Sometimes we need to say, "Holy Spirit, what is really going on here?"

You can't tap out of this match, but you can tap into God's thought patterns and exchange your thoughts for His. There was a time in my life when it would appear that my mind was my greatest enemy.

Fencing Master

Where there is unity there is always victory.[2]

—Publilius Syrus, Latin writer

More often than not, I entertained any and every negative thought that came around. These thoughts visited me in my sleep, invaded my dreams, and interrupted time with my husband. Fearful thoughts of rejection and suspicion kept me from making friends, just as surely as they separated me from the friends I already had. They exhausted, isolated, accused, abused, and then—in some perverse way—affirmed me. How? Negative thoughts can become self-fulfilling prophecies.

I knew I couldn't trust her...

I knew there was something wrong there...

Your children would be better off with a different mother...

Your husband doesn't really love you...

You never finish any thing you start...

You're a lazy procrastinator...

I've had all of these invasive thoughts regularly visit my mind. Sometimes they would bring along their sisters, brothers, and cousins. These visitors voiced thoughts that sound shockingly similar to those that came before them.

4 | I know you have had some of these visitors as well. Right now, without overthinking it, what uninvited thought has bombarded your mind lately?

_____

_____

_____

_____

_____

The hope of the enemy is that if you hear something long enough, you will begin to believe it, granting these thoughts permission to gain expression for themselves through your words and actions.

Take my list, for example. Let's examine the friendship dynamic. Distrust of others may mean I was never the kind of friend I should have been. If I'm afraid someone is going to rob or betray me, on some level, I will guard myself—when what is necessary for the health of both parties is that I give of myself. Of course, you must choose wisely and give what is healthy and pure. For example, you can always know it is safe to encourage others towards godliness, wisdom, and kindness. You never give away your heart or soul. Even in marriage we merge to become one. We don't lose ourselves; we find ourselves in another facet.

Our enemy wants to divert our focus from the unseen wrestling match so that we are distracted and controlled by a shadowed expression of evil. He doesn't want to see us strike at the source that is actually casting the shadow. Attempting to defeat the enemy by wrestling with people could be likened to trying to destroy a tree by picking all its fruit. To kill a tree, you must destroy the root system.
[Page 54]

In most cases, he is after our thoughts!

Recently I read that *overthinking* leads to depression. I have absolutely no doubt about this. God has a remedy for this:

> *Seek the Lord while he may be found; call upon him while he is near; let the wicked forsake his way, and the unrighteous man his thoughts; let him return to the Lord, that he may have compassion on him, and to our God, for he will abundantly pardon. **For my thoughts are not your thoughts, neither are your ways my ways, declares the Lord. For as the heavens are higher than the earth, so are my ways higher than your ways and my thoughts than your thoughts.***
> Isaiah 55:6-9

Living in the dark, alone with a bunch of negative thoughts, will make you crazy! I know because there have been times when I have reasoned myself straight into the realm of the ridiculous—and so can you. The answer to this is that God's Word gives us the ability to think God's thoughts. This is the very reason we must renew our minds with the Word of God.

> *Throw off your old sinful nature and your former way of life, which is corrupted by lust and deception. Instead, let the Spirit renew your thoughts and attitudes. Put on your new nature, created to be like God—truly righteous and holy.*
> Ephesians 4:22-24, NLT

We strip off our former nature and ways by renewing our thoughts and attitudes. How? By thinking, speaking, and then living by the sword of God's Word.

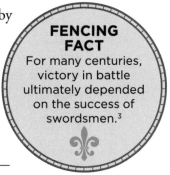

FENCING FACT

For many centuries, victory in battle ultimately depended on the success of swordsmen.[3]

If our *true* enemy is unseen then that enemy can't be numbered among people (because we can see them). Believe me, I know it feels like people are your enemies, and some truly are— but they are **not** the driving force!

Something a bit more cunning and ancient has you in its sights. I believe the serpent-dragon fears what you carry.

5 | What might that be?

_____

_____

_____

_____

_____

_____

_____

Just as labors precede natural birth, there are temporal battles before eternal dreams. Individually, we are His dream fought for and won. Then collectively (male and female, young and old), we are the dragon's worst nightmare! This is a big reason God wants us united:

> *I do not ask for these only, but also for **those who will believe** in me*
> ***through their word**, that they may all be one, just as you, Father,*
> *are in me, and I in you, that they also may be in us, so that the world may*
> *believe that you have sent me. The glory that you have given me I have*
> *given to them, that they may be one even as we are one, I in them and*
> *you in me, **that they may become perfectly one**, so that the world*
> *may know that you sent me and loved them even as you loved me.*
>
> John 17:20-23

Jesus was praying for us. He included you and I in the number who would one day believe because of His disciples. Through the Scriptures, we watched them walk with Jesus, run from Him, and return to bring Him glory. Just as Jesus needed their lives and words to be a testimony that would show Him to us, the time has come for us to reveal Jesus to others.

6 | This means others will believe because of you! So lovely one, who believes because of you?

_____

_____

_____

_____

_____

_____

Fencing Master

The unity of Christendom is not a luxury, but a necessity. The World will go limping until Christ's prayer that all may be one is answered.[4]

—Charles H. Brent

It's time we were all answers to Jesus' prayer.

The fulfillment of this prayer has not happened yet, because we are certainly not yet one. *One* does not equate to *same*. To be one we must actually be different. But don't mistake *different* for divisive and divided! Our current behavior toward one another causes many to question all that we stand for. The Message maps out John 17:23 this way:

*I in them and you in me. Then they'll be mature in this oneness, and give the godless **world evidence** that you've sent me and loved them in the **same way you've loved me.***

United, there's a chance the world might yet believe.

Sparring
Questions for group discussion

G

7 | Are we acting as though God sent His Son to save the lost world, or do we behave in a way that says it is all about us?

8 | Do we sing songs that include the lost, or do they only talk about how God is related to us?

a | Do we believe God loves them in the same way He loved Jesus?

9 | Is it hard for you to imagine that the Father loves you just as He loved His heavenly Son?

When this portrayal of *one* heart and mind is seen, the next verse tells us what will happen:

> *Father, I want those you gave me* **to be with me, right where I am**,
> *so they can see my glory, the splendor you gave me,*
> **having loved me long before there ever was a world.**
> John 17:24, The Message

You are a gift God created for His Son!

10 | How does this make you feel?
- **A.** Uncomfortable and apprehensive
- **B.** Unworthy and condemned
- **C.** Elated and expectant
- **D.** Like buried treasure waiting to amaze Him!

We are a mystery hidden in Christ waiting to be revealed on that day!

> *Making known to us the mystery of his will, according to his purpose,*
> *which he set forth in Christ as a plan for the fullness of time,*
> *to unite all things in him, things in heaven and things on earth.*
> Ephesians 1:9-10

Heaven and earth meet in Christ. Jesus came in the fullness of time, and we walk the earth as time wanes. Perhaps this is the very hour for the Church to be at its fullest.

Fencing Master

We are each other's harvest; we are each other's business; we are each other's magnitude and bond.[5]

—Gwendolyn Brooks

Full stature would mean one heart, one voice, one vision, one purpose, one name, one kingdom, and one mandate to glorify Jesus. Then our weary earth will glimpse heaven.

11 | What areas of the Body would you presently describe as…

a | Full stature?

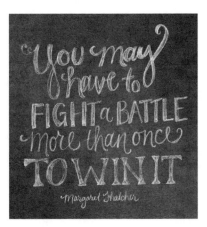

You may have to FIGHT a BATTLE more than once TO WIN IT

—Margaret Thatcher

b | Half stature?

c | No stature?

12 | How can you help these areas fill and mature?

Fencing Master

There are a thousand hacking at the branches of evil to one striking at the root.[6]

—Henry David Thoreau

Work for Peace

Peace means work. Peace in your marriage requires work. A house full of children means a work of peace. It is a lot of work, but it's work He blesses!

> *God blesses those who work for peace,*
> *for they will be called the children of God.*
> Matthew 5:9, NLT

Division happens without any labor. If you want peace, you must work. Since the fall of man, discord and division are the natural course of this world. Unity and peace require intentional and strategic wisdom. If they are to come, it means we must employ heaven's actions to counter our culture's initiatives.

Fencing Master

Satan always hates Christian fellowship; it is his policy to keep Christians apart. Anything which can divide saints from one another he delights in.[7]

—Charles Spurgeon

13 | Why does Satan divide?

_____

_____

_____

_____

Division never glorifies Jesus. Discord divides hearts, homes, voices, vision, purpose, and kingdoms. Division has many faces: pride, rage, wrath, contention, slander, gossip, curses, strife, bitterness and offense, witchcraft, and idolatry (see Galatians 5:19–21). These affronts gain access to our world when we live by the carnal or brute human instincts. Even though divisiveness has many faces, it ultimately has a singular goal: our destruction.

[Page 58]

But if you have bitter jealousy and selfish ambition in your hearts, do not boast and be false to the truth. This is not the wisdom that comes down from above, but is earthly, unspiritual, demonic. For where jealousy and selfish ambition exist, there will be disorder and every vile practice.

James 3:14-16

I have often heard people ask why there is so much sin in the Church. The verse above gives us our answer:

*For where jealousy and selfish ambition exist, there will be disorder and **every vile practice**.*

Hello, here we are! Jealousy and selfish ambition are the antithesis of oneness, and vile practices are running rampant through our ranks. If we stop the one, we will stop the other.

Jesus conquered death, hell, and the grave so that He could be one with us. It is time to be one with one another. Some of the most powerful relationships are forged when iron crosses iron and the resulting friction sharpens both. More often than not, you will encounter the greatest resistance to unity as soon as you intentionally decide to walk in it.

Marriage, families, and churches—all of these institutions are set up to make us one:

Marriage isn't a promise to always be in love; it is a promise to always love.

Family isn't about always agreeing; it is about always being there for one another.

Churches are to be of one heart and mind, but that doesn't mean we will always meet in the same building.

What began with division between Adam and Eve ends with the unity of Christ and His bride.

*"There is no neutral ground in the universe;
every square inch, every split second, is claimed
by God, and counter-claimed by Satan."*
—C.S. Lewis

14| What do you think this means?

_____

_____

_____

_____

_____

_____

The dragon purposefully divides, demeans, and discourages any who would hope to rise up and move into the light by daring to dream in the dark.

Lovely One, if you dare to dream you must be brave enough to fight.

Maybe when you were a little girl, the dragon spoke words of fire that turned your hopes to ashes.

15| Did you know you would have to fight to realize your dreams?

_____

_____

_____

_____

a| What is a dream you had to fight for?

_____

_____

_____

_____

_____ ⚜

Maybe he twisted words until you imagined his thoughts were your own. Did someone say you were ugly, fat, skinny, flat, stupid, too smart, short, or tall?

16 | Does the concept of your being a treasure seem absurd?

_____

_____

_____

_____

_____

Sword Words

Counterclaim this with:
I am fearfully and wonderfully made!
Psalm 139:14

Maybe your parent's love turned to hate, and the former shelter of your home turned into an empty shell of a house.

17 | Deep down, are you afraid your marriage (present or future) will never last because you are damaged goods?

_____

_____

_____

_____

_____

Sword Words

Counterclaim this with:
Also, since you are Christ's family, then you are Abraham's famous "descendant," heirs according to the covenant promises.
Galatians 3:29, The Message

Maybe someone rode the dragon's wings in the night and came to you in the dark and touched you in places and ways that made you feel ashamed and dirty. Maybe as the serpent of shame slithered away, he hissed, "You asked for this; you wanted this; you are the one who made me do this."

Sword Words

Counterclaim this with:

Keep your eyes on Jesus, who both began and finished this race we're in. Study how he did it. Because he never lost sight of where he was headed—that exhilarating finish in and with God—he could put up with anything along the way: cross, shame, whatever. And now he's there, in the place of honor, right alongside God.

Hebrews 12:2, The Message

Because we do not wrestle with people, blame is always a distraction from what is truly going on. Any pain caused by people is just a shadow puppet of what is behind the scenes: a thieving dragon-serpent who must be struck with a sword.

We fight for the dream: a people who are one, with the glory of God operating openly in their lives. When we are the answer to Jesus' prayers, we flourish.

The following scripture astounds me:

> ***At that time* GOD** *will unsheathe his sword, his merciless, massive, mighty sword. He'll punish the serpent Leviathan as it flees, the serpent Leviathan thrashing in flight. He'll kill that old dragon that lives in the sea.*
> ***At that same time**, a fine vineyard will appear. There's something to sing about! I, GOD, tend it. I keep it well-watered. I keep careful watch over it so that no one can damage it.*
>
> Isaiah 27:1-3, The Message

18 | Could this "at that time" be realized when we are one?

_____

_____

So lovely hero, let your roots go down deep. Draw your strength from the unseen and never allow the shadowed form of the dragon to blight the light of your future.

Sword Play

Sword sisters fight for each other! As a group, decide how you will increase peace and unity in your midst—then act on what you say!

Room for Reflection

_____

_____

_____

_____

_____

Fencing Lessons

- ⚜ Our conflict exists on the unseen battlefield of the spirit.
- ⚜ Negative thoughts and overthinking are strategies for division.
- ⚜ When we are united, the world will believe in His love.
- ⚜ You are a gift God prepared for His Son!
- ⚜ If you want to dream, you must be willing to fight.

SKILL CHECK
What God defines we should not redefine, and what He joins we should not separate.

En Garde

The most powerfully heroic thing you can do is to be fruitful.

Impressions

(1) "Christian spiritual warfare quotes," DailyChristianQuote.com, accessed February 21, 2013, http:// dailychristianquote.com/dcqspiritwarfare.html. (2) "Publilius Syrus quotes," ThinkExist.com, accessed February 9, 2013, http://thinkexist.com/quotation/where_there_is_unity_there_is_always_victory/149280.html. (3) "About the sport," Swordsport.com, accessed February 21, 2013, http://www.swordsport.com/sport.html (4) "Unity quotes," oChristian.com, accessed February 4, 2013, http://christian-quotes.ochristian.com/Unity-Quotes/. (5) "Quotes about Unity," Goodreads.com, accessed February 4, 2013, http://www.goodreads.com/quotes/tag/unity. (6) "Henry David Thoreau quote," QuotationsBook.com, accessed March 12, 2013, http://quotationsbook.com/quote/45330/. (7) "Unity Quotes," oChristian.com, accessed February 4, 2013, http://christian-quotes.ochristian.com/Unity-Quotes/page-4.shtml.

The Cross as
a Sword

Of all the chapters in this book, perhaps this is the most important one of all. It's time we delve a bit deeper into the wonder of the cross, because without this knowledge we will never truly know what it means to be in Him. In keeping with this goal, this chapter will be content-heavy.

The Blood deals with what we have done,
*whereas the Cross deals with **what we are.***
The Blood disposes of our sin, while the Cross
***strikes at the root of our capacity** for sin.*
—Watchman Nee

1 | How does the cross address *what we are*?

_____

_____

_____

_____

_____

_____

(G) 2 | How does the cross strike *the root of our capacity?*

_____

_____

_____

_____

_____

_____

3 | In one word what does the cross mean to you?

_____

a | Does your word appear in the collection that came through my social media avenues?

_____

The cross bridged the gaping chasm between heaven and earth to reconcile God and man and went on to transform what appeared to be horrific defeat into stunning triumph. This empowering hope of transformation has spanned the ages.

No other victory was compelling enough to reach back and light mankind's dark history, while at the same time extending its rays into all that we know as future.

4 | How often do you hear the cross preached?

_____

_____

_____

*The conquest of the cross was more than timeless—it **is** eternal.*

a | How often do you think about the cross?

_____

_____

_____

_____

It is worthy of more than an annual Easter pageant appearance. Let's intentionally visit the cross now:

Close your eyes and imagine rough pieces of wood artificially joined to form a wooden cross. Notice that once it is erected, it looks strangely like a makeshift sword with its point planted in the ground.

Now imagine our Jesus—God's very Word made flesh, the glorious Son—with His naked, beaten body stretched the length of this horrid sword blade. Nine-inch nails anchor His hands to the cross-guard, and behind our master's head is the wooden sword's grip.

5 | Do you see this likeness between the cross and a sword?

_____

_____

_____

_____

Jesus' broken body hung like fruit from this dead tree.

Grasping at equality with God, Adam tasted the stolen fruit of a beautiful but forbidden tree; therefore all within Adam die.

Stripped of His divine privileges, Jesus tasted death and gave His life as our fruit on a barren tree, that *in Him* all might live.

> ## Fencing Master
>
> The life Christ lived qualified Him for the death He died—and the death He died qualifies us for the life we live.[1]
>
> —Unknown

Are you awestruck by what Jesus has done for us? We are no longer trapped in the curse of Adam. We are hidden in Christ and bound to a promise backed to the hilt.

> *When God made his promise to Abraham, **he backed it to the hilt**, putting his own reputation on the line.... When God wanted to guarantee his promises, he gave his word, a rock-solid guarantee—God can't break his word. And because his word cannot change, the promise is likewise unchangeable.*
> Hebrews 6:13, 17–18, The Message

Hilt

Fencing Term

Hilt: handle of a sword consisting of pommel, grip, and cross-guard.

God used the cross as a sword to put to an end the hostility Adam created between God and man.

Jesus' death on the cross was God's promise to Abraham (and his heirs), kept to the uttermost.

Who Was Responsible for the Cross?

6 | Have you heard Satan blamed for the crucifixion?

a | Who else have you heard blamed?

"But when the tenants saw the son, they said to themselves, 'This is the heir. Come, let us kill him and have his inheritance.' And they took him and threw him out of the vineyard and killed him. When therefore the owner of the vineyard comes, what will he do to those tenants?" They said to him, "He will put those wretches to a miserable death and let out the vineyard to other tenants who will give him the fruits in their seasons."

Jesus said to them, "Have you never read in the Scriptures:
"'The stone that the builders rejected
  has become the cornerstone;
this was the Lord's doing,
  and it is marvelous in our eyes'?

Therefore I tell you, the kingdom of God will be taken away from you and given to a people producing its fruits. And the one who falls on this stone will be broken to pieces; and when it falls on anyone, it will crush him."

*When the chief priests and the Pharisees heard his parables, **they perceived that he was speaking about them.***
Matthew 21:38-45

7 | So who killed Jesus, and what was the motivation?

_____

_____

_____

8 | Have you seen dramas that portrayed the resurrection as a big surprise?

_____

_____

a | Were you surprised by how open Jesus was about the resurrection plan?

_____

_____

> *"You know that after two days the Passover is coming, and the*
> *Son of Man will be delivered up to be crucified."*
>
> *Then the chief priests and the elders of the people gathered in the palace*
> *of the high priest, whose name was Caiaphas, and plotted together*
> *in order to arrest Jesus by stealth and kill him.*
> Matthew 26:2–4

9 | The religious leaders thought that by killing God's Son they would get to steal His inheritance, but what actually happened?

_____

_____

_____

_____

> *None of the rulers of this age understood this, for if they had,*
> *they would not have crucified the Lord of glory.*
> 1 Corinthians 2:8

10 | Who were these rulers?

_____

_____

_____

11 | What blindsided each and every ruler of that age?

_____

_____

Fencing Master

All God's plans
have the mark of
the cross on them.[2]

—E.M. Bounds

These rulers could not see the transforming and triumphant power of the cross. Crucifying Jesus didn't steal the Son's inheritance. Through His death we became His inheritance. What they tried to rob, they actually became!

> *Yet among the mature we do impart wisdom, although it is not a wisdom of this age or of the rulers of this age, who are doomed to pass away. But we impart a secret and hidden wisdom of God, which **God decreed before the ages** for our glory.*
> 1 Corinthians 2:6-7

Before our foolishness, God's wisdom was at work. Before time was birthed, God thought of you.

(G) 12 | What does that say about your value?

_____

_____

_____

The cross was woven into heaven's mysterious tapestry of eternal wisdom. This magnificent rendering of His love continuously unfolds and reveals itself.

Think of it:

*Jesus was our Lamb **before** sheep were created...*
*Savior of our earth **before** the world was founded...*
*We were chosen to be spotless "in Him" **before** our sins made us scarlet!*

> *...even as he chose us in him before the foundation of the world, that we should be holy and blameless before him.*
> Ephesians 1:4

Before Eden was seeded, we were planted in Him. **Before** Adam and Eve were put out of the garden, we were securely hidden in Christ.

Satan and the rulers of that age did not realize that as Jesus came up out of the grave, we rose with Him!

Sword Words

I have been crucified with Christ. It is no longer I who live, but Christ who lives in me. And the life I now live in the flesh I live by faith in the Son of God, who loved me and gave himself for me.
Galatians 2:20

Jesus didn't just take our place. He gave us His—His life, His name, His words, His authority, and His promise. Just as in Adam all have sinned, in Christ all are forgiven. Our lives, hidden in Christ and crucified with Christ, are mysteries He longs to unveil!

You see, the cross was always part of the plan. It was not a backup plan that was set into motion when Adam and Eve failed. It is the fail-safe.

*For **in him we live, and move, and have our being**; as certain also of your own poets have said, For we are also his offspring.*
Acts 17:28 KJV

He is our life, our author, and the One who changes us. We exist because of Him. The exchange on the cross shifted us from death in Adam to life in Christ. Even though we walk the earth, we are seated with Christ.

Jesus' death was not a surprise. The resurrection was not a shock. But the fact that as He rose we'd been quickened as well was what blew their minds!

So glorious a Father of love is our God that He not only forgave, but also adopted as His very own, those guilty of murdering His Son. I don't know if I could do this—but in Him, we actually could. What are you afraid of facing? In Him, you can!

Review Matthew 16:21-23.

I love that Peter wanted to protect Jesus; normally this would be a great motive. But it didn't work because he was,

*...seeing things **merely from a human** point of view, not from God's.*
verse 23 NLT

There it is again: in Christ, we have a new vantage!

13 | What is a challenge you are presently facing that you might be seeing "merely from a human point of view"?

_____

_____

_____

_____

_____

The Power of Before

We were saved, forgiven, healed, loved, graced, empowered, and restored "in Christ." Just as "in Christ" God caught us <u>before</u> we fell. The mystery and wonder of it will forever unfold.

Eternity alone will reveal the brilliance of the cross.
[Page 71]

The following list is but a glimpse into this brilliance:

Before there was an adversary, a garden, a man, a woman, and a serpent, there was an answer.
Before there was a war, there was a victory.
Before there was even the concept of a game, the cross was the game-changing agent.
*He made a way for you **before** you lost yours.*
*He loved and knew you long **before** you knew and loved Him.*
*God covered us **before** we realized we were naked and made us whole **before** we knew we were broken.*

(G) 14 | Write your very own "before" here:

_____

_____

_____

_____

_____

The cross was the means that facilitated the purpose for which Jesus was born. It was the dead tree that brought us all back to life. He lifted you in Christ long before you stumbled. Our Giver of all Life changed the cross into a tree of life.

(G) 15 | Why the cruel cross?

_____

_____

_____

_____

_____

16 | How did the cross accomplish the croisé?

FENCING FACT

The croisé: this move works by leveraging a hostile opponent's aggression back upon him, and in the process the foe is disarmed.

_____

_____

_____

_____

_____

_____

_____

_____

Our magnificent Savior took the blade when His side was pierced, but on the cross He took upon Himself the hostility of all the ages. What should have been devastating proved to be disarming. On the cross God leveraged all that He is for all that we could be.

Leverage works best with the least amount of resistance. This is the reason Jesus was like a Lamb led to the slaughter. He laid down His life without a struggle because He had fully entrusted it to His Father. Jesus yielded His soul to God and His body to His enemies—and the cross of Christ became the lever that saved the world.

> *Give me a lever, and I will move the world.*
> —Archimedes[3]

Ultimately sword fighting is not a contest of strength; it is one of finesse and strategic endurance.

> *But now in Christ Jesus you who once were far off have been brought near by the blood of Christ. For he himself is our peace, who has made us both one and has broken down in his flesh the dividing wall of hostility by abolishing the law of commandments expressed in ordinances, that he might create in himself one new man in place of the two, so making peace, and might reconcile us both to God in one body through the cross, thereby killing the hostility.*
> Ephesians 2:13–16

Hostility had been alive since Adam. The cross eradicated every trace of it and made us one.

In Christ, men and women are one flesh.
In Christ, Jews and Gentiles are woven into one vine.
In Christ, the Old and New Testament saints become one cloud of witnesses.
In Christ, we are at once contained and uncontainable.

TRAINING DRILL
I challenge you to highlight the phrase "in Christ" every time you see it in the New Testament. Let it remind you where you truly stand.

After God raised us up with His Son, He filled us with the same Spirit who raised Christ from the dead so that every decaying area of our lives could be regenerated and redeemed.

> *The Spirit of God, who raised Jesus from the dead, lives in you.*
> *And just as God raised Christ Jesus from the dead, he will give life*
> *to your mortal bodies by this same Spirit living within you.*
> Romans 8:11 NLT

He became like us so we could be like Him. In Him a great mystery is expressed and somehow we all become one.

> *And I will give them one heart, and a new spirit I will put within them.*
> *I will remove the heart of stone from their flesh and give them a heart*
> *of flesh, that they may walk in my statutes and keep my rules and*
> *obey them. And they shall be my people, and I will be their God.*
> Ezekiel 11:19-20

Lessons from the Cross:

✠ In Christ, the many share one heart.

✠ In Christ, all that was divided becomes unified.

✠ In Christ, the far off, lost, and wandering come near.

✠ The cross is the ultimate assurance of every promise kept.

Scapegoat: one that bears the blame for others.[4]

17 | Before you realized the wonder of "in Christ," did you ever feel like a scapegoat?

_____

_____

_____

_____

_____

_____

None of this should trouble you any longer, because Jesus has a space for you. All of us are flawed, but He is flawless. There is no longer need for any scapegoats, because Jesus took it all. The blood of Christ brought "in" all who had wandered and purged any remnant of shame that tried to isolate and keep us as scapegoats.

> *Yet it was our weaknesses he carried; it was our sorrows that weighed him down. And we thought his troubles were a punishment from God, a punishment for his own sins! But he was pierced for our rebellion, crushed for our sins. He was beaten so we could be whole. He was whipped so we could be healed. All of us, like sheep, have strayed away. We have left God's paths to follow our own. Yet the Lord laid on him the sins of us all.*
> Isaiah 53:4-6 NLT

Jesus did nothing to deserve punishment, and we did nothing to deserve His sacrifice. He was rejected, betrayed, pierced, crushed, and beaten—whipped, oppressed, and then crucified.

The rulers of the age thought the cross was Jesus' end; they had no idea it was their beginning. The cross is the sword of love.

Isn't it time you carried it?

Sword Play

Each of us carries a special revelation in our experiences of the cross. Take some time as a group to discuss each of your answers to the question, "In one word what does the cross mean to you?" (page 64)

Room for Reflection

_____

_____

_____

_____

_____

_____

_____

Fencing Lessons

- The utterly obedient sacrifice of our Christ saves to the uttermost.
- The cross is the sword that put to death every trace of hostility between heaven and earth, just as surely as it is a sword that transforms us through the surgery of the Word.
- The cross was your hope even before you realized you were hopeless, the answer before you realized there was a problem.
- Through the cross we are equipped to walk in Him.

SKILL CHECK
On the cross, God backed His promises to the hilt and caught us long before we even fell.

En Garde

The cross symbolizes God's faithfulness while also expressing His faith in us.

Impressions

(1) "The Cross quotes," Tentmaker.org, accessed February 9, 2013, http://www.tentmaker.org/Quotes/thecrossquotes.htm. (2) Ibid. (3) Nick Evangelista, The Art and Science of Fencing (Lincolnwood, IL: Masters Press, 1996), 126. (4) "Scapegoat," Merriam-Webster Dictionary, accessed February 21, 2013, http://www.merriam-webster.com/dictionary/scapegoat.

6

Becoming a Warrior

It is better to have the opportunity of victory, than to be spared the struggle.
—Amelia E. Barr[1]

1 | Why does a warrior fight?

2 | What is the way of the warrior?

(G)   a | What does "freedom without fear" mean to you?

Terrorists are driven by fear, mercenaries and soldiers of fortune are motivated by greed, and even enlisted soldiers *must* obey commands.

3 | What separates the warrior from those listed above?

_____

_____

_____

_____

_____

_____

_____

Lovely one, you were born for this season of upheaval, conflict, and war. The enemy's attacks range from the intimate atrocities of child abuse and abandonment in our homes to insidious networks that traffic twenty-seven million for sex and labor.[2] In addition to these dark, secret terrors there are open threats as nations challenge each other with the threat of depersonalized war.

Never forget your power of choice. Each day you can choose what you will serve: fear and hatred, or love. We cannot choose our time period or family, and there are times we cannot choose our battles—but we *always* have the power to choose *how* we will fight.

Choose this day to fight each battle in such a manner that will ultimately and gloriously win the war. Dare to believe that choosing nobly in the small and seemingly insignificant will put you well on your way to being a warrior.

It isn't just actions that move ahead with us into the future; the lessons we learn on each path journey with us as well. If you planted well in the last season, you will see the fruit in a future season.

Warriors understand that what was challenging in their last season was meant to build strength in their future.

4 | Remind yourself of a time when you saw this dynamic played out in your life.

Warriors in Heaven!

5 | Were you surprised to hear that there are warriors in heaven?

It stands to reason that if there are swords in heaven, there must be warriors; and if there are warriors, it must mean there is war.

> *Cush was also the ancestor of Nimrod, who was*
> *the **first** **heroic warrior on earth.***
> Genesis 10:8, NLT

Our troubled world is a fallen, shadowed reflection of the exalted, glorious heavens. This means that conflicts waged long ago in heaven become apparent and exert themselves on our earth.

> *Now **war arose in heaven**, Michael and his angels fighting against*
> *the dragon. And the dragon and his angels fought back, but he was*
> *defeated, and there was no longer any place for them in heaven.*
> Revelation 12:7-8

The defeated were displaced from heaven, and they brought war to our earth. Review the following passage from Revelation 12:

> *And when **the dragon** saw that he had been thrown down to the earth,*
> ***he pursued the woman** who had given birth to the male child. But the*
> *woman was given the two wings of the great eagle so that she might fly from*

the serpent into the wilderness, to the place where she is to be nourished for a time, and times, and half a time. The serpent poured water like a river out of his mouth after the woman, to sweep her away with a flood. But the earth came to the help of the woman, and the earth opened its mouth and swallowed the river that the dragon had poured from his mouth. Then the dragon became furious with the woman and went off to make war on the rest of her offspring, on those who keep the commandments of God and hold to the testimony of Jesus. And he stood on the sand of the sea.
Revelation 12:13-17

The Church is a *feminine* term that includes *both* male and female—yet the dragon's fury is *repeatedly* leveled against "the woman." First Eve, then Sarah, then Israel, then Mary. Now his venomous attacks are leveled at the Bride, and there is no surer way to wound a woman than to attack her children. And who are the children of this woman? *All* who keep God's commands and hold to the testimony of Jesus.

You are already a target. You might as well choose to be a warrior hero.

Our Father Lord is a Warrior

Again, as I use the terms *warrior* and *soldier* in this chapter, I am not referencing those who so selflessly serve in our nation's armed forces. Instead, I employ these words in order to frame the motivation we daughters of God should hold as we engage in this battle. For truly our heavenly Father is a warrior:

> *The LORD is a warrior; Yahweh is his name!*
> Exodus 15:3 NLT

And again in the English Standard Version,

> *The Lord is a man of war; the Lord is his name.*
> Exodus 15:3

You are his daughter and thus a warrior; it is time you stopped acting like an enslaved soldier.

Life is a collection of seasons, and each new season adds a new level of training. First you discover that there is an order to things. For example, He is our Father: He gives the orders and assigns authority according to our positions. And you always first learn to follow orders before you are allowed to give them.

It is important that we discern where and when we are behaving like warriors or soldiers. Later in this chapter you will have the opportunity to practically evaluate your current level of mastery in these areas. But first, let's begin by reviewing the contrast from the book:

Warriors are called. Ultimately you are a royal daughter of the King, hand-chosen for a purpose. There is nothing impersonal about this battle; it is an all out war on your family.

Soldiers are hired through enlistment or draft. You are not a civilian who has been drafted or hired as part of a passing conflict in a distant land; this is your ancient battle.

Warriors are moved by compassion. There is a quickening within that joins them to the cause.

6 | What quickens or moves you?

_____

_____

_____

_____

_____

Warriors are honorable. This way of fearless honor begins in the heart and works its way out into our lives. We honor our Lord by behaving honorably toward others. Soldiers honor rank; warriors honor all.

While most soldiers are paid, true warriors are made.

Soldiers are trained. Warriors are tempered. Training comes through practice, but tempering comes under pressure.

Soldiers know what the enemy is doing; warriors know what God is doing.

Warriors are driven by an internal eternal mandate. They know their Father's heart, not just His orders. Soldiers follow the order to the letter but lose the heart of it along the way. The letter kills, but the Spirit knows how to give life.

FENCING FACT

Tempering a blade is the process of improving both the hardness and elasticity of the metal by reheating and then cooling it, often more than once.[3-4] The word *temper* also holds another meaning: to make stronger and more resilient through hardship.[5] (More on this in the next chapter.)

Good men must not obey the laws too well.
—Ralph Waldo Emerson

7 | What do you think Emerson meant by this?

_____

_____

_____

_____

_____

Soldiers have an enlisted mindset. When their time is up, they are gone. They hold their position, but their position has no hold on them. They serve so they can retire.

Warriors never retire. *Warrior* is a posture one carries throughout life. King David was a warrior from beginning to end! Here is an example from early in his life:

David said to Saul, "Your servant used to keep sheep for his father. And when there came a lion, or a bear, and took a lamb from the flock, I went after him and struck him and delivered it out of his mouth. And if he arose against me, I caught him by his beard and struck him and killed him."
1 Samuel 17:34-35

Warriors understand all victories begin in private. They know that our God *never* wastes a private victory. What if David had chosen not to kill the lion or the bear? What if he had decided one sheep wasn't worth risking his life? A soldier resolves to keep a better watch in the future, but **warriors understand the future is now**. This is why warriors go after the thief and recover all.

Never imagine that what you do for others or what you do in private doesn't matter. It counts more than we know. God watches how we steward what is not our own before He entrusts us with more. A warrior doesn't weigh the odds when right needs to triumph over wrong. It takes the heart of a warrior to pursue a lion with a lamb in its mouth. The battles we win in private position us to slay giants in public.

8 | Remember a victory you won in private. What lessons and skills were gained?

_____

_____

_____

_____

_____

_____

_____

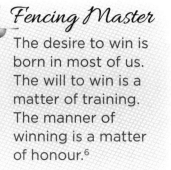

Fencing Master

The desire to win is born in most of us. The will to win is a matter of training. The manner of winning is a matter of honour.[6]

—Margaret Thatcher

David's greatest warrior moments were captured in the stories of who he let live. Warriors understand they carry a sword for the sake of justice, not judgment. All soldiers can kill; it takes a warrior to let an enemy live.

Warriors fight according to the will of God, while soldiers war for the will of the people.

Warriors speak bold words of faith and take action; soldiers give status reports. **Warriors know there is no need to number the enemy when you have a revelation of who fights with you!** Soldiers fear men and obey people. Warriors fear the Lord and obey God. Even if you've come from a long line of soldiers, the spirit of a warrior resides within you!

9 | What issues of legacy have caused you to believe you cannot be a heroic warrior? (These could include family history of divorce, depression, etc.)

_____

_____

_____

_____

a | What truth would God's Word bring to dismantle any arguments against our warrior destiny?

_____

_____

_____

Like Jonathan, you must be brave enough to leave behind what is not working. Dare to find victory in unexpected places (like the enemy's camp). It's time to take a risk and find another way.

Sword sister, you will come out of this womb of tempering drawing a breath of strength. We warriors allow pressure to change our name from _soldier_ to _warrior_, from servant to daughter. Outward pressure is always an opportunity to be inwardly transformed.

> Warriors never imagine they've been hired to do a job, because they know they are called to change their world.

Warriors learn to trust the whispered call deep within, while soldiers feel pressured to respond to the noise that surrounds them.

Soldiers and warriors process pressure in different manners. Soldiers will adopt an endure-or-escape approach. They do things to relieve the pressure: eat, drink, run, raid or pillage, shop —anything to take the mind off the conflict. It is the very reason that soldiers under constant and cruel pressure retaliate with cruelty. What they are under works its way into them and gains expression.
[Page 99]

Fencing Master

God does not give us overcoming life; He gives us life as we overcome.[7]

—Oswald Chambers

Warriors respond by allowing the pressures around them to increase the pressure level within them until there is balance.

Warriors are seasoned by the battles of life, while soldiers fight for just a season in life.

Are You a Soldier or a Warrior?

This test will assess the skill with which you wield your weapon. Answer each question honestly, for only from a position of humility can we be raised up (see James 4:10). Remember, every soldier can become a warrior. Invite the Spirit to bring His powerful grace and train you in areas where you lack mastery.

	Soldier	Warrior
Fighting this spiritual battle is...	[ ] an obligation	[ ] a matter of honor
What matters most to me is...	[ ] the position I hold	[ ] how well I fulfill it
I would say that I am...	[ ] battle weary	[ ] energized by the cause
I follow...	[ ] my King's orders	[ ] my King's heart
In everyday life, my filter is...	[ ] the way things are now	[ ] what God can do
I care...	[ ] that I win	[ ] how I win
I celebrate victory...	[ ] when it brings recognition or praise	[ ] in every battle, public or private
Studying the Scriptures...	[ ] is optional for my lifestyle	[ ] is something I must and desire to do
I mostly consider...	[ ] my own interests	[ ] the interests of God's kingdom
I value the Word...	[ ] when I am in seasons of pressure, transition, or hardship	[ ] in every season, regardless of circumstance
I view God's principles and promises...	[ ] as old-fashioned or unrelated to my life	[ ] as highly relevant to my life, relationships, family, etc.
I am more influenced by...	[ ] popular opinion or spiritual "trends"	[ ] God's unchanging, eternal truth

10 | Which of these do you find most challenging? Why?

_____

_____

_____

_____

_____

_____

_____ ❖

Our Tale of Two Kings

We close this chapter by contrasting Israel's first king, Saul, and her final and forever King, Jesus.

> *Saul said to Samuel, "I have sinned, for I have transgressed*
> *the commandment of the Lord and your words, because*
> *I feared the people and obeyed their voice."*
> 1 Samuel 15:24

God had placed Saul head and shoulders above the people so they could look up to him, but instead Saul stooped to their level. He was an insecure leader who measured his worth by what the people said about him. Jesus never sinned and thus never transgressed the commandment of the Lord. He did not obey the voice of people because He delighted in the fear of the Lord.

There is nothing more debilitating than the fear of man. King Saul died as he lived: afraid of what others might do to him. In contrast, there is nothing more freeing than the fear of the Lord. Our warrior King Jesus died as He lived: knowing what the people would do to Him.

Sword Words

What scripture(s) bring perspective when you face the fear of man? Record them here:

The cross teaches us that there is no greater weapon than a life laid down. No one took the life of Jesus. He gave it. Jesus refused deliverance and relief so He could be both to us. Rather than fall upon a sword, He carried the cross.

> *When he sees all that is accomplished by his anguish,*
> *he will be satisfied.*
> *And because of his experience,*
> *my righteous servant will make it possible*
> *for many to be counted righteous,*
> *for he will bear all their sins.*
> *I will give him the honors of a victorious soldier,*
> *because he exposed himself to death.*
> Isaiah 53:11-12, NLT

God will always grace and strengthen us to do His will. You are the daughter of a triumphant warrior king. Walk in all the honor, virtue, courage, beauty, loyalty, and freedom this represents.

Sword Play

A true warrior cares for what is not her own as if it were. This is especially powerful in the workings of God's Bride, the Church. As a group, discuss how you can support the vision of your pastor or leader.

Room for Reflection

Fencing Lessons

- ❖ God is the original warrior!
- ❖ The way of the warrior is freedom without fear.
- ❖ Warriors and swords both have their origin in the eternal.
- ❖ Warriors judge by what is unseen and make bold moves in faith.
- ❖ Soldiers fear men, but warriors fear and serve the Lord.
- ❖ Every soldier can become a warrior.
- ❖ God never wastes a private victory.
- ❖ There is no greater weapon than a life laid down.

En Garde

You are the daughter of a triumphant Warrior-King.

SKILL CHECK
Soldiers fight for a season in life, but warriors are seasoned by the battles of life. Soldiers are paid; warriors are made.

HEROES are always brave, BUT DON'T IMAGINE THAT always brave translates to never afraid

····Lisa Bevere
➤➤GIRLS WITH SWORDS···

Impressions

(1) "9 Rules for Success by British Novelist Amelia E. Barr, 1901," BrainPickings.org, accessed February 11, 2013, http://www.brainpickings.org/index.php/2013/02/05/9-rules-for-success-by-amelia-barr/. (2) "Trafficking in Persons Report," June 2008, http://www.state.gov/documents/organization/105501.pdf, 7. (3) "Temper," Oxford Dictionaries, accessed February 22, 2013, http://oxforddictionaries.com/definition/american_english/temper. (4) "How Sword Making Works," HowStuffWorks.com, accessed February 22, 2013, http://science.howstuffworks.com/sword-making6.htm. (5) "Temper," Merriam-Webster Dictionary, accessed February 22, 2013, http://www.merriam-webster.com/dictionary/tempering. (6) "Margaret Thatcher quotes," ThinkExist.com, accessed February 11, 2013, http://thinkexist.com/quotation/the_desire_to_win_is_born_in_most_of_us-the_will/289440.html. (7) "My Utmost for His Highest quotes," Goodreads.com, accessed February 22, 2013, http://www.goodreads.com/work/quotes/1559310-my-utmost-for-his-highest-traditional-updated-edition-my-utmost-for-hi.

7

Forging a Sword

Hard times don't create heroes. It is during the hard times when the "hero" within us is revealed.
—Bob Riley

I certainly agree with this quote: hard times can be revealing—but there are times when hardship brings out the worst rather than the best. Pressure reveals our core. This is ultimately a good thing. If I'm an idiot, a coward, or a crazy person under pressure, I'd rather find out now and fix that break before it breaks me!

(G) 1 | How is the process of crafting a sword similar to forging a life?

_____

_____

_____

_____

_____

To shore up our weak places and refine our strengths, God uses some serious forces like water, fire, and a hammer.

The process of sword making is not altogether different from that of weaving. Once heated, that which was stiff becomes pliable enough to braid and twist, thus creating a tension that fuses the separate strands into the whole. Then the woven metal visits the crucible of fire yet again to be heated and cooled and hammered and stretched.

Fencing Master

Heat is required to forge anything. Every great accomplishment is the story of a flaming heart.[1]

—Arnold H. Glasgow

*This dance between extremes is a process known as **tempering**.*

Tempering produces swords that are strong yet flexible. Through it, rods are molded and then twisted together until there is no telling where one begins and another ends. Next come hammering, shaping, and polishing before a blade appears and is ready to be attached to a hilt, which likewise must have been processed and tempered in order for it to be handled.

Likewise, God uses the elements of fire, water, and pressure to refine His daughters in order to transform our weakness into strength, our rigidity into flexibility. He hones a shapeless life into one of sharp and focused purpose.

2 | What is your favorite thing about water?

_____

_____

_____

a | When does water frighten you?

_____

_____

_____

3 | What is your favorite thing about fire?

_____

_____

_____

a | What is it about fire that frightens you?

_____

_____

_____

_____

4 | What levels of pressure do you enjoy or perform well under?

_____

_____

_____

_____

_____

_____

Fear not, for I have redeemed you; I have called you by name, you are mine. **When** *you pass through the waters, I will be with you; and through the rivers, they shall not overwhelm you;* **when** *you walk through fire you shall not be burned, and the flame shall not consume you.*
Isaiah 43:1–2

Isaiah 43 starts out happily: *Don't be afraid. I'm your redeemer. I know your name because you are Mine.* Then it all goes downhill from there. Notice the word choice in this passage is *when*, not *if.* There *will* be waters and rivers, as well as fire and flames. But our safe passage through these is guaranteed. It truly helps if we realize we are not alone in this process and He has promised to bring us through!

5 | Give an example of a time you passed through water:

_____

_____

_____

_____

_____

6 | Give an example of your traveling through flames:

_____

_____

_____

_____

_____

For a sword to function properly, in addition to being *tempered*, it must be balanced. A sword is balanced according to its use. Without proper balance, a sword is at best ineffective; at its worst, an unbalanced sword is dangerous. Blacksmiths strive for something called *harmonic balance* when they create a sword; this refers to how the sword will carry the vibration that results from a strike.

Passages through fire and water—the experiences of undergoing pressure— serve to balance our lives.

FENCING FACT

Center of balance (CoB): The center of balance (also known as the center of gravity or point of balance) is the point along the blade where the sword possesses equal mass on either side.[2]

7 | I loved learning that samurais balanced their aggressive natures with flower arranging. Likewise, David balanced his with worship and songwriting. How can you add some balance to yours? For example, if you are naturally gentle, what might you do to temper that strength? If you tend to be more on the aggressive side, what might bring balance to your nature? If all you focus on is the serious, maybe you should add in some humor.

_____

_____

_____

_____

_____

_____

_____

_____

Cards & Spankings

When one of my sons was visiting some friends, they asked how we had raised him up to be such a balanced young man. His answered surprised them. He said it was a combination of playing cards and sound spankings.

In case you haven't already guessed, John and I run on the intense side of the street. This means we have to play with the same intensity. We forced our children to engage in games with us. Our basement resembles an arcade: it's home to ping pong, video games, and foosball. At our house we pray hard and play hard. We yell and laugh loudly, and we sleep and eat soundly.

> *Behold, I have refined you, but not as silver;*
> *I have tried you in the furnace of affliction.*
> *For my own sake, for my own sake, I do it,*
> *for how should my name be profaned?*
> *My glory I will not give to another.*
> Isaiah 48:10-11

This charge to *behold* is an invitation to look at something from a larger, vaster vantage.

Whenever we are in "the process," we can lose sight of the purpose. You have no idea you are being balanced, refined, and tempered. You just think you are passing through the four-letter name for the underworld! For clarity, God tells us this refining is for His sake.

Good things are not necessarily pain free.

8 | Define *affliction*:

_____

_____

_____

_____

_____

9 | Record the last time you went through affliction and the fruit it produced.

_____

_____

_____

_____

_____

It's important that you remember the good that came out of it because...

**There's more to come:** We continue to **shout our praise** even when we're hemmed in with troubles, because we know how **troubles** can **develop passionate patience** in us, and how that patience in turn **forges the tempered steel of virtue**, keeping us alert for whatever God will do next. In alert expectancy such as this, we're never left feeling shortchanged.
Romans 5:3-5, The Message

More battles require more swords. Each sword must be tempered and balanced. Each battle can make you or break you. If it breaks you, the metal goes back into the fire and the water and then returns under the hammer to be tempered again.

(G) 10 | In your own words, define _passionate patience._

_____

_____

_____

_____

_____

_____

_____

_____

_____

⚔ _Fencing Master_

Opportunities to find deeper powers within ourselves come when life seems most challenging.[3]

—Joseph Campbell

11 | What are the two types of afflictions we all experience? (See page 111.)

_____

_____

_____

(G) 12 | What happens when things get uncomfortable?

_____

_____

_____

> "This is as true in everyday life as it is in battle:
> we are given one life and the decision is ours
> whether to wait for circumstances to make up our
> mind, or whether to act, and in acting, to live."
> —General Omar N. Bradley[3]

En Garde

Today I choose to act and thus live, rather than allow the battle to drive me.

Lessons achieved through hardship are the most valuable because they are the most personal. It is through hardship that life puts your faith to the pressure test:

> Consider it a sheer gift, friends, when tests and challenges [**affliction**] come at you from all sides. You know that under pressure [**forging**], your faith-life is forced into the open and shows its true colors. So don't try to get out of anything prematurely. Let it do its work [**tempering**] so you become mature and well-developed, not deficient in any way [**balance**].
> If you don't know what you're doing [**since I don't know what I'm doing**], pray to the Father. He loves to help. You'll get his help, and won't be condescended to when you ask for it. Ask boldly, believingly, without a second thought. People who "worry their prayers" are like wind-whipped waves. Don't think you're going to get anything from the Master that way, adrift at sea, keeping all your options open.
> James 1:2-8, The Message

13 | What might your current afflictions be attempting to forge in your life?

_____

_____

_____

_____

a | What areas need to come into balance?

_____

_____

_____

14 | What environment is God creating for you now (think about the flowers in my refrigerator drawer) so that you might bloom later in every season?

_____

_____

_____

Pray the kind of prayers that scare what is scared inside you! If your prayers aren't scaring you, then they certainly are _not_ scaring the enemy!

Sword Words

What is the battle you are currently facing? Is there a promise in God's Word that is your answer? Using scripture, construct a scary prayer and write it down:

Fencing Master

Persistence is to the character of man as carbon is to steel.[4]

—Napoleon Hill

Remember, swords may have two edges, but they are never double-minded! As you step out in faith, stand your ground. Once you strike, don't draw back: see it through to the end!

Will you choose to allow adversity and affliction to refine, temper, sharpen, and balance you, or will you crumble? The following is my slightly altered, personalized version of 1 Thessalonians 1:4-5:

*It is clear to me, lovely sister and friend, that **God not only loves you very much but also has put his hand on you for something special**. When the Message we preached came to you, it wasn't just words. Something happened in you. **The Holy Spirit put steel in your convictions**.*
1 Thessalonians 1:4-5, The Message with author's paraphrase

15 | What might God have put His hand on you for? (If you are unsure, ask Him. He wants you to know!)

_____

_____

_____

_____

_____

_____

_____

_____

_____

_____

_____

_____

_____

Lovely one, NO LONGER think of yourself as T·A·R·G·E·T·E·D
YOU WERE FIRST CHOSEN TO BE A sword LIFTED IN HIS HAND. Live like a hero AND YOU WILL STRIKE A SURE BLOW TO THE ENEMY and captives WILL BE set free

Sword Play

Think of someone in your world who is in a season of tempering. Select a few scriptures to bring as bold, believing prayers over her life every day this week. (Involve this friend in the faith process if you can.)

Room for Reflection

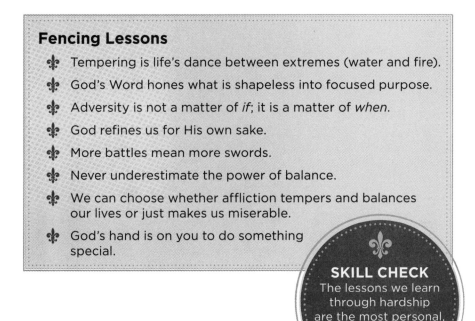

Fencing Lessons

❖ Tempering is life's dance between extremes (water and fire).

❖ God's Word hones what is shapeless into focused purpose.

❖ Adversity is not a matter of *if*; it is a matter of *when*.

❖ God refines us for His own sake.

❖ More battles mean more swords.

❖ Never underestimate the power of balance.

❖ We can choose whether affliction tempers and balances our lives or just makes us miserable.

❖ God's hand is on you to do something special.

SKILL CHECK
The lessons we learn through hardship are the most personal, and this makes them the most valuable.

(1) "Arnold H Glasgow quote," ThinkExist.com, accessed February 13, 2013, http://thinkexist.com/quotation/nothing_splendid_was_ever_created_in_cold_blood/297106.html (2) "Basic Sword Terminology," Albion Swords, accessed February 25, 2013, http://www.albion-swords.com/swords/sword-terms.htm. (3) "Joseph Campbell quote," iWise.com, accessed March 13, 2013, http://www.iwise.com/eSL14. (4) "Napoleon Hill quote," BrainyQuote.com, accessed February 13, 2013, http://www.brainyquote.com/quotes/quotes/n/napoleonhi152868.html.

Impressions

8

Sword Words

For though we walk in the flesh, we are not waging war according to the flesh. For the weapons of our warfare are not of the flesh but have divine power to destroy strongholds.
2 Corinthians 10:3-4

Sometimes as I read these words, I wonder, *Do we really know what we have at hand?* This divine weapon we hold is empowered to destroy strongholds.

The saber we've been entrusted to bear is not lifted with our hands; it is raised by our words. We speak the Word of God as a weapon heard long before it is ever seen.
[Page 121]

You and I draw forth our swords by the words we choose to speak. We must intentionally speak as ambassadors of faith, hope, and His love. It is better to remain silent than to draw a sword at the wrong time or on the wrong person. If we don't know what to say, we have the Word of God as our life scripts, and we are charged to wield it with grace.

All Scripture is inspired by God and is useful to teach us what is true and to make us realize what is wrong in our lives. It corrects us when we are wrong and teaches us to do what is right. God uses it to prepare and equip his people to do every good work.
2 Timothy 3:16–17, NLT

All Scripture has the potential to teach, correct, prepare, and equip us. When we edit what we live out loud, we run the risk of finding ourselves ill-equipped and unprepared, not unlike a woman who leaves home with toothpaste on her face because she neglected to check her reflection before heading out the door.

Scriptures act like a mirror, changing us so we reflect what is true and deflect what is false. They also have the power to change our reflection: beneath the scalpel of the Word we are renewed and unveiled.

1 | What are some areas of your reflection that you would like to see transformed?

a | **Spirit:**

_____

_____

_____

b | **Soul:**

_____

_____

_____

c | **Body:**

_____

_____

_____

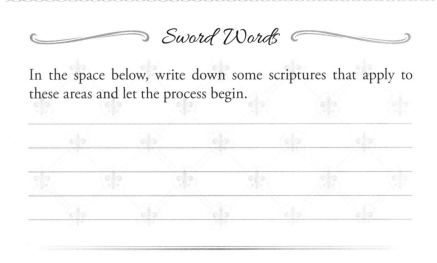

Sword Words

In the space below, write down some scriptures that apply to these areas and let the process begin.

_____

_____

_____

_____

_____

Our Father's Language

Do you remember the film *My Fair Lady*? In this classic, Audrey Hepburn was transformed from a guttersnipe to the very image of a lady by changing the way she spoke the English language.

Right or wrong accents can say a lot about a person. People use them to determine if you are a foreigner, rich or poor, "one of us" or an outsider.

> *He who comes from above is above all. He who is of the earth*
> *belongs to the earth and speaks in an earthly way.*
> John 3:31

Language has the power to elevate or demean, bless or curse, heal or wound. We can speak after the manner of this earth or after the pattern of heaven. The Message paraphrases John 3:31 this way:

> *The One who comes from above is head and shoulders over other*
> *messengers from God. The earthborn is earthbound and speaks*
> *earth language; the heavenborn is in a league of his own.*

The way you speak tells others where you are from. You were earthborn, but now you are heaven-born. I am not advocating that we all learn Hebrew, but I am advocating that we restructure what we say to heaven's language.

FENCING FACT
Fencing has a language of its own that combines Italian, French, English, and more.

There are benefits in learning a second language: improved cognitive reasoning and problem-solving, as well as increased executive brain function and even prevention of dementia! And that is just an earthly language!

Heaven is our eternal home; doesn't it make sense to learn its language now? It is time we speak the language of our rebirth, of our Father's land.

My heart is stirred by a noble theme as I recite my verses for the king;
my tongue is the pen of a skillful writer.
Psalm 45:1, NIV

This is obviously an admonishment to do more than read; *recite* usually involves memorization, and your tongue is not involved unless you use it to form the words you read. This type of recital isn't simply an art form. God wants to display His power in and through you. By removing the limits of the structure and motivation of human language, we are attached to the purpose of the league of heaven's heroes.

In this manner, prayer becomes a divine intervention because we are no longer limited to our human perspective. The Word gives us a vantage that is "head and shoulders" (God's governance) above what rules this earth. We lift our swords when we lift His Word. "It is written" causes the earth to shift and darkness to tremble.

Death and life are in the power of the tongue.
Proverbs 18:21

This is the very reason it is crucial we submit our words to heaven's authority.

2 | What are some current areas of "darkness and death" that you need to speak God's Word of life and light into?

_____

_____

_____

God's words are flawless and vibrant. They are likened to our living swords that light the darkness. He has entrusted His children with a powerful, holy, ancient language. These living words should be used honorably. When His holy words are misused or wielded in angry judgment, the reflection is twisted, and heaven's light is marred by darkness…. The heady combination of shared language and purpose has the power to connect people of all ages and gender and the inhabitants of all nations in a magnificent way.

When I wrote the book *Nurture,* I framed this attribute as a language of the heart that women hold in common. Languages can express themselves in both verbal and nonverbal ways. Nurture is an example of our common mother tongue, as surely as our native language expresses the national origin of our birth.

As important as both of these are, with this message I hope to unearth another layer. I want to delve a bit deeper and speak of a language even more powerful than the language of our native origins or our heart's mother tongue. The very words of this language are woven with the substantive power to move the unseen into the seen and create something out of nothing.

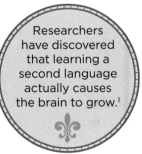

Researchers have discovered that learning a second language actually causes the brain to grow.[1]

When our Father spoke, creation was set in motion. Out of a dark void of shapeless chaos, order and light burst forth. If we are going to be awed daughters who do awe-inspiring things to honor our awesome God, we need His words and name.

> *Out of the abundance of the heart the mouth speaks.*
> Matthew 12:34

Like our Heavenly Father, we see our thoughts released and often realized by what we speak.

This scripture in Matthew is usually referenced as an admonition to guard our hearts or to take stock of what is stored up in them, listening to what comes out of our mouths to be assured that no bad things come forth. But let's look at this scripture through a different lens, because out of the abundance of God's heart, He spoke the universe of galaxies into existence.

For his invisible attributes, namely, his eternal power and divine nature, have been clearly perceived, ever since the creation of the world, in the things that have been made.
Romans 1:20

Fencing Master

We inhabit a language rather than a country.[2]

—Emile M. Cioran

You are even more exciting and complex than oceans, mountains, and lions! You, lovely one, reflect an attribute of our invisible God.

When the language of heaven is whispered, vast distances are instantaneously spanned, and the realms of earth and heaven are unified. And it is ours to speak because it is the language of our Father.

3 | What positive, healing things might you intentionally begin to speak? (For example: love in your marriage, destiny for your children, or unity for the Church.) Write some ideas here:

_____

_____

_____

_____

_____

_____

I cannot overemphasize this: the Holy Scriptures are the living, breathing language of your true home. As such, each sentence is filled with imagery and instructions.

His Word supersedes all that we've ever known as language, because his words were the genesis of all we now see.
[Page 126]

The amazing news is that this language is not like the French or other earthly tongue. Our Father's language can be flawlessly spoken by everyone! These powerful, ancient texts are available to every tribe and dialect.

A Common Tongue

During the incident at the Tower of Babel, God scattered a disobedient people who shared a common language, because He warned:

*And nothing that they propose to do will now be impossible for them.
Come, let us go down and there confuse their language,
so that they may not understand one another's speech.*
Genesis 11:6-7

The impossible becomes possible because of two factors: a *united people* and a *shared language.*

4 | What current trends that would have been impossible in the past are now becoming the norm because of united people and language?

_____

_____

_____

_____

_____

_____

The story of our human existence began with one language, and it will end with one language: a language of the wonder of God.

At this sound the multitude came together, and they were bewildered,
because each one was hearing them speak in his own language.
And they were amazed and astonished, saying, "Are not all these who
are speaking Galileans? And how is it that we hear, each of us in his
own native language? Parthians and Medes and Elamites and residents
of Mesopotamia, Judea and Cappadocia, Pontus and Asia, Phrygia and
Pamphylia, Egypt and the parts of Libya belonging to Cyrene, and
visitors from Rome, both Jews and proselytes, Cretans and Arabians—
we hear them telling in our own tongues the mighty works of God."
Acts 2:6–11

5 | The point here is not whether you personally speak in tongues or not.
I believe the point is, do you use your tongue to declare God's wonder?

_____

_____

_____

_____

6 | How divisive has this issue of speaking in tongues been for you?

_____

_____

_____

Ⓖ   a | Do you believe it is something worth dividing over?

_____

_____

_____

_____

Multitudes will always gather when heaven finds voice on earth. When
we truly have something to say, God finds a way to interpret it for all who
need to hear. When we yield ourselves to speak His words by the power
of His Spirit, astonishing things can happen. I believe women will lead
the way in this unified expression of God's wonder.

Even more important than sharing a common earthly language that sounds the same is the collective power of saying the same thing. On the day of Pentecost, the declarations of heaven invaded earth, and all who were present knew it.

7 | Do you believe the Church has focused on the wrong things?

a | What are some ways we can better glorify God?

8 | Will we speak in our flawed manner or tell of His flawless works? Explain the difference:

Will we be a unified voice by allowing His Spirit to fill us?

9 | I have never seen a commitment to unity work unless all participants were aligned with a higher cause. What give us this?

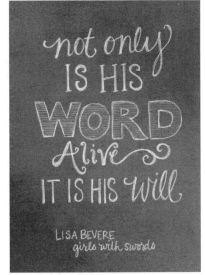

not only
IS HIS
WORD
Alive
IT IS HIS will

LISA BEVERE
girls with swords

The truth is this: At best we only know our part—in part! To understand the function of a part, it is best to have an idea of the image of the whole.

Missing pieces would naturally mean that there are parts we know...and other parts where the Spirit and the Word of God fill in the blanks. We prophesy and speak a word of faith to create substance for what we've yet to see of the other part. He is our all in all; we are part of a whole.

[Page 129]

10 | For far too long the Word has been interpreted rather than proclaimed. What is the difference?

_____

_____

_____

_____

11 | Do you agree that we've passed the Word through the filter of our human experiences, social preferences, current prejudices, and the limited counsel of the human mind?

_____

_____

12 | What areas of the Word have you drawn back from?

_____

_____

_____

_____

_____

Flip the Switch

On the day of the *Girls with Swords* book release, I did a conference call with many of the women who were part of the launch team. I learned that many of them did not know they could be bold with the Word. They second-guessed their ability to teach the Word, train their children, and even pray the Word, simply because they were women. Is it only for the sons to speak the words of their Father?

Fencing Master

The limits of my language means the limits of my world.[3]

—Ludwig Wittgenstein

So my sisters whispered, hinted, interpreted, or remained silent rather than simply declaring what was so powerfully and eternally spoken and recorded. (But not anymore!)

Man or woman, it takes faith to declare a language we do not understand.

> *By faith we understand that the worlds have been framed*
> *by the word of God, so that what is seen hath not*
> *been made out of things which appear.*
> Hebrews 11:3, ASV

We understand that God framed the world we see by words we cannot see, but we don't necessarily understand how that happened. The truth is, there are a lot of things we don't understand, but we still use them! I don't completely understand electricity, but I do know how to change a light bulb, flip on a switch, and plug in and unplug devices. My lack of "understanding" electricity completely does not keep me from accessing it, but it does make me respect it. In the case of God's Word, our fear of the Lord could be likened to our respect for the power of electricity.

As we act like our Father and echo His words, the sword finds its substance, just as surely as flipping on a switch makes power possible. The created earth recognizes His words and aligns itself to the will of its Creator.

13 | Are there scriptures you've been afraid to believe or promises that you've been afraid to trust because you didn't understand them?

_____

_____

_____

a | What do you need to flip the switch on and connect with today?

_____

_____

_____

_____

I understand you may feel that it is wrong to use the Word of God to get things; but the truth is, we need to use the Word of God to do things, and doing things involves…things! (By "things" I mean relationships, resources, etc.) Our wisdom is best drawn from the Ancient of Days rather than from the people of our day.

> *"Who is this that hides counsel without knowledge?"*
> *Therefore I have uttered what I did not understand,*
> *things too wonderful for me, which I did not know.*
> Job 42:3

We question His greatness when we dull the edges of His heavenly Word.

> *Preach the word; be urgent in season, out of season; reprove, rebuke,*
> *exhort, with all longsuffering and teaching. For the time will come*
> *when they will not endure the sound doctrine; but, having itching ears,*
> *will heap to themselves teachers after their own lusts; and will turn*
> *away their ears from the truth, and turn aside unto fables.*
> 2 Timothy 4:2–4, ASV

Rather than preach light words, preach words of light! I understand there was a season in the past when the sword of God's Word was spoken without light, or in legalism. Human agenda always distorts the brilliance of God's Word.

In order not to frighten people, many ministers and leaders pulled back, and in an attempt to be seeker-sensitive, they added a derivative language. I think seeker-sensitive methods are great, but we make a mistake when we allow our methodology to compromise God's message.

Catchphrases are easy to remember because they are so catchy, but if the words are not eternal, they will not catch you when you fall.

14 | How have avenues of social media contributed to this problem of "light words"?

_____

_____

_____

_____

(G)   a | What can we do to use these sources correctly?

_____

_____

_____

In our desire to be all things to all people, we cannot lessen the weight of the holy. I pray we are not creating a generation of wise fools who know everything and do nothing.

Warnings

Why do we imagine the invitation to *selah* (be still and awed by wonder) was inserted so frequently throughout the psalms? When asked what his concerns were for the next century, William Booth said:

> In answer to your inquiry, I consider that the chief dangers which confront the coming century will be religion without the Holy Ghost, Christianity without Christ, forgiveness without repentance, salvation without regeneration, politics without God, and heaven without hell.[4]

(G) 15 | Where do you feel we are in light of William Booth's warning?

_____

_____

_____

_____

_____

Now is not the time to divide camps and point fingers. The condition of the body of Christ is too desperate. If what we have declared over the last few decades created this current reality, let's be intentional about constructing a new framework built on the solid rock of God's Word. Let's speak God's wisdom and watch the healing begin.

How many of you saw the 2010 film *Alice in Wonderland*? In it, nineteen-year-old Alice returns to Wonderland to slay a fierce dragon known as the Jabberwocky. Before she confronts her enemy, she must retrieve the Vorpal Sword, the only weapon capable of killing this foe. It's interesting that when Alice found herself facing the Jabberwocky, he didn't fear her. But he was afraid of what she held:

"**Jabberwocky:** So my old foe, we meet on the battlefield once again.
Alice: We have never met.
Jabberwocky: Not you, insignificant bearer: my ancient enemy, the Vorpal one."

The same is true of us. What we hold in our hands overshadows our human inadequacies. The enemy sees what we bear, not what we've been.

16 | To put this in practice, what are some things you can pray to bring balance back into your own life?

_____

_____

_____

_____

_____

_____

_____

_____

_____

Our words begin to echo the will of our Father in heaven, and the vineyard begins to flourish.

God's living Word is the origin of all the powerful, transformative truths. Ultimately, the Truth is not a theory to be debated; He is the Word made flesh: Jesus.

> *Jesus said to him, "I am the way, and the truth, and the life.*
> *No one comes to the Father except through me."*
> John 14:6

There's a vast difference between telling the truth and being the truth! We are to follow Jesus' example of living the truth. He is the truth without an expiration date, because He is alive forevermore! One "truth" encourages you in the moment; the other transforms you with its light and momentum.

Not only is His Word alive; it is His will. How can I say this? Because Jesus showed the will of the Father, and He is God's Word expressed in human flesh.

> *Consequently, when Christ came into the world, he said,*
> *"Sacrifices and offerings you have not desired, but a body have you*
> *prepared for me; in burnt offerings and sin offerings you have*
> *taken no pleasure. Then I said, 'Behold, I have come to do your will,*
> *O God, as it is written of me in the scroll of the book.'"*
> Hebrews 10:5–7

So the question arises—what is written of us in the scroll of the book?

I believe His will is often found in the very scriptures that burn in your heart. Lay hold of these and speak them out loud in love and boldness!

As we begin to read and apply all the Word, and not just our favorite passages, then we will truly recognize what has been placed in our hands. The body of Christ will rise united when we use our strengths to hone rather than to attack one another. As the Church submits to God's washing and correction, she will remember that swords are used on enemies, not friends.

Sword Play

Be aware of any inspiring concepts or phrases that capture your mind and heart this week (through social media, teaching, conversation, or even your own thoughts). Take some time to discover what God's Word says about them. Record both the phrases and their eternal source in the space below.

_____

_____

_____

_____

_____

Room for Reflection

_____

_____

_____

_____

Fencing Lessons

⚜ All Scripture is designed to teach, correct, prepare, and equip.

⚜ How you speak reveals where you are from.

⚜ God's Word has the power to invite the unseen into the seen.

⚜ God's Word must be proclaimed, not interpreted.

⚜ Swords are used on enemies, not friends.

⚜ The impossible is possible for a united people with a shared language.

SKILL CHECK
As earthborn beings reborn for heaven, it is time we learn to speak the language of our Father's land.

En Garde

God's daughters will be part of the heaven-breathed outpouring of His Spirit.

Impressions

(1) "Language learning makes the brain grow," AlphaGalileo Foundation, accessed February 15, 2013, http://www.alphagalileo.org/ViewItem.aspx?ItemId=124679&CultureCode=en. (2) "Emile M. Cioran quote," BrainyQuote.com, accessed February 15, 2013, http://www.brainyquote.com/quotes/quotes/e/emilemcio181760.html. (3) "Ludwig Wittgenstein quote," BrainyQuote.com, accessed February 15, 2013, http://www.brainyquote.com/quotes/quotes/l/ludwigwitt138017.html. (4) Pete Brookshaw, "The Greatest Challenges Facing the Salvation Army Today," www.petebrookshaw.com/2012/07/greatest-challenges-facing-salvation.html, July 1, 2012.

9

Sword of Harvest

*Look, I tell you, lift up your eyes, and see
that the fields are white for harvest.*
John 4:35

Even though it is extremely versatile, I wish our North American soil had produced something a bit more romantic than the machete. Then again, harvest is not a time for epic sword fighting; it is a time to work.

1 | List the four main purposes of the machete:

_____

_____

_____

_____

As you now know, when you clear paths, people find their way; when you change environments, you create refuge; when you harvest fields, you enjoy the fruit of your labor—but when you do all these things, you run the risk of encountering snakes.

Clearing and Maintaining Paths

When I held the conference call with the women who were part of the *Girls with Swords* launch team, one of them shared how she wanted to hear a bit more about the dynamic of ways and paths. So let's start with some definitions.

Ⓖ 2 | Drawing from *Girls with Swords* and other resources, define *path*:

_____

_____

a | According to scripture, how many paths are there?

_____

Over the course of time, paths can become overgrown, littered, and lost. The shadow of our day may obscure its entrance, but we are promised an entrance.

> *The entrance of thy words giveth light; it giveth*
> *understanding unto the simple.*
> Psalm 119:130, KJV

You are not limited to the light levels of this earthly environment. As God's Word enters your heart, you are "enlightened" in the truest sense. What was formerly dangerous in the dark is exposed and therefore dealt with in the light.

I want to give an example of this here. Let's say someone was wrestling with an addiction to pornography. The hold of this addiction grows stronger the longer it lives in the shadows. But when it is brought to the light (such as being examined in the light of God's Word) and then confessed to a friend, steps can be taken to kill what grew strong in the shadow realm.

Conversely, the "light" of this world would call the darkness of pornography...light. The world would say things like, "Watching porn together will enrich your marriage," or, "It will keep you from cheating." When this kind of reasoning takes place, the light within you becomes darkness and you stumble off course onto the wrong path until light finds you again.

New and Ancient Paths

God is asking us to forge new trails by reopening ancient paths. *Ancient* does not mean *old* as much it means timeless and eternal. Grace does not discredit the holy. Far too many have wandered off the highway of holiness (see Jeremiah 18:15). We know He is the Lord our God who *makes* us holy; this transformation is not a license for us to act unholy. More than ever we need His Word in order to clear paths in the wild so we can find our way out of the dark. The sword of God's Word has the power to sever what entangles us.

> *...delivering you from the **way of evil**,*
> *from men of **perverted speech**,*
> *who forsake the **paths of uprightness***
> *to walk in the **ways of darkness**,*
> *who rejoice in doing evil*
> *and delight in the perverseness of evil,*
> *men whose **paths are crooked**,*
> *and who are **devious in their ways**.*
> Proverbs 2:12–15

In the last chapter we learned that language has the power to elevate, so it should come as no surprise that it likewise can demean. Perversity of speech eventually leads to perverse ways and crooked paths. Continuing on these courses will ultimately separate you from the way of life. This scripture shows three things:

evil has a way, a path, and a language

...just as we already learned that righteousness has a way, a path, and a language.

A sampling of evil's methods or ways would include pride, disobedience, dishonor, slander, perversity, lying, fornication, adultery, idolatry, vengefulness, hate, envy, wrath, witchcraft, and manipulation.

A sampling of the ways of life can be found in Galatians 5:22-23: love, joy, peace, patience, kindness, goodness, faithfulness, gentleness, and self-control.

To review: the term *path* differs from *way* because *way* is the manner in which you travel and *path* is the course to where you are headed.

Fencing Master

If we all tried to make other people's paths easy, our own feet would have a smooth even place to walk on.[1]

—Myrtle Reed

3 | Give examples of literal *ways* of travel:

_____

_____

a | Give examples of literal *paths*:

_____

_____

In context of the Scriptures, the way of traveling righteous paths is by telling the truth rather than lying, which brings us once again to the dynamic of language.

Language has the power to connect and transport us to righteous paths and ways, just as surely as our words have the power to separate us from evil—the way being *how* we journey, and the path being the route or *where* we are going.

4 | What are some of the reasons that sincere people have been misled?

_____

_____

_____

Do not go where the path may lead, go instead where there is no path and leave a trail.

Ralph Waldo Emerson

(G) 5 | Do you agree that there are times that the righteous path requires unconventional approaches?

_____

_____

_____

> *Jesus never diverted from the path of righteousness, but he was definitely a trailblazer.*
> [Page 144]

He commissioned us to do the same when He sent us to make disciples in every nation. Jesus ate with sinners and spoke to a dysfunctional Samaritan woman. He was not typical in His day. After His death, things became even more radical: salvation was offered to the Gentiles!

(G) 6 | Name some of your favorite radicals who have not left off the path of righteousness.

_____

_____

_____

The very way you begin to leave the path (perverse talk) reveals the way to return to it (righteous talk). By reading God's Word, we will learn His ways; and by speaking His language, what we seek opens up before us. Through the power of His Word, He makes a way where there seems to be no way.

Let's rephrase Psalm 119:28-32 as our prayer,

Heavenly Father,
*Barricade and block any of the roads that would take me **Nowhere.***
*I am tired of traveling the empty and dark paths. Grace me now with Your clear revelation. I want to see things the way You do. This day I choose the true road to **Somewhere.***
As I travel this road, I will post Your road signs at every curve and corner so that those who follow me will not fall or falter. I will speak Your Word and grasp and cling to whatever You tell me; God, You've

never let me down! I'm ready to run the course You lay out for me. I am ready; show me the way.
Amen.
Your daughter

To get this process started, you will want to be mindful of new words you need to say as well as conversations you may need to leave. Make some notes here:

_____

_____

_____

Change Environments

The Word not only has the power to light our environment, but it can change it as well. Fasting, prayer, and declaring the scriptures can literally increase your inner capacity. Sometimes enlarging what is within us means disengaging from what is around us.

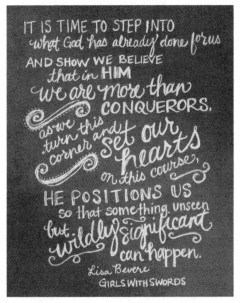

We do not meditate to have a better knowledge of ourselves but to have a deeper revelation of God within us. I have never been able to change by looking at my own reflection. Change happens when I turn from myself, look at Him, and do what He says. Jesus normally then points me to other people rather than back to the mirror.

Why Environmental Change is Good

Last night I hosted fifty young women in my home. Afterward they lingered and shared their stories of struggle. Each of them has such a sense of God destiny, but they are unsure how to express this purpose. One shared that when she is around ministry leadership she feels a constant undercurrent of containment: not one of guidance and training but of control. It sounded as though there was an unspoken understanding that *she was allowed to walk this far and in this manner, but no further.* She wasn't even sure exactly where these boundaries began or ended, just that they were in place, and that if she crossed them it would mean trouble. She asked me if I ever felt that way, and if so, did I ever say anything?

I explained to her that in the past I remained quiet. Whenever I felt I was being devalued or diminished I stepped back a few feet. I shared that I used to speak in questions, afraid to say anything too strongly because I didn't want to get hit with the backlash. But in the last few years all that has changed. I had strong male and female leadership tell me to knock it off. This admonishment pushed me into some new environments, the very ones that appreciate answers more than questions.

I also began to realize that what I left unanswered and in place (condescending attitudes) would maintain a difficult environment for the daughters and women who would come in after me. I could dance around the thorn bushes or use my machete to cut away briars.

I have learned to stand in my position always aware that it is an honor and with respect for the entrustment. The truth is that fearful cowering does not communicate respect to anyone. Knowing who you are and respecting who others are is what we need. The Word of God tells us who we are and cuts away what we are not.

The most persuasive argument you will ever make is the one you make with your life.

We displace evil with good, darkness with light, lies with truth, despair with hope, fear with love, and death with life. We use the Word to take ground and establish our entrusted areas with a new lifestyle and environment.

7 | What environment might God be asking you to change?

_____

_____

_____

Behold, I have given you authority to tread on serpents and scorpions, and over all the power of the enemy, and nothing shall hurt you. **Nevertheless, do not rejoice in this, that the spirits are subject to you, but rejoice that your names are written in heaven.**

Luke 10:19–20

FENCING FACT
A good fencing school discourages elitism and values learning over competition.[2]

We are not to rejoice because of what is subject to us; we rejoice because our names are written in another realm that is high above. We use our authority to walk on top of what is under us so that we remember what is before us.

8 | How might you use God's Word to create refuge, shelter, and even places of storage and abundance for others?

_____

_____

_____

_____

Manage Harvests

Do you not say, *"There are yet four months, then comes the harvest"?* ***Look, I tell you, lift up your eyes, and see*** *that the fields are white for harvest. Already the one who reaps is receiving wages and gathering fruit for eternal life, so that sower and reaper may rejoice together. For here the saying holds true, "One sows and another reaps." I sent you to reap that for which you did not labor. Others have labored, and you have entered into their labor.*

John 4:35–38

Notice how this begins with Jesus asking, *"Do you not say...?"* Then He shifts their vantage to, *"Look, I tell you, lift up your eyes, and see..."* He was shifting their eyes from what they had known to a harvest they could but only imagine. What they saw said, "It is not time yet." What Jesus saw said, "There's a harvest of righteousness!" I believe that by speaking the Word, the eyes of our understanding will be enlightened!

Harvest is a short season of urgency. All that we hold in our hands must be wielded for more than one purpose. The same word that will clear paths can harvest grain, just as the same sword that can create shelter may have to kill snakes. In the same way, our resources should be for both shelter and harvest, for path clearing and defense. Our days could be likened to the days of Nehemiah who defended as he built. Likewise we defend as we harvest.

Sword Words

Proclaim this among the nations: Consecrate for war;
stir up the mighty men. Let all the men of war draw near;
let them come up. Beat your plowshares into swords, and your
pruning hooks into spears; let the weak say, "I am a warrior."
Joel 3:9–10

Say it: **I am a warrior!**

You are truly a warrior, but it is important that we are on constant guard in remembering that we are co-laborers, not competitors. Just as Jesus and John the Baptist refused to be part of the Pharisees' competition, you must do the same. Satan will try to pit us against one another so he can throw us all in a pit. Don't let him!

All of us should adopt the attitude of John. Forerunners do not split the playing field; they prepare the way! We have the privilege of announcing the One to come, not the scores of the players. Competition is a very human response, but as you've already learned, we are raising the level above what is merely human.

Fencing Master

Nothing is ever done beautifully which is done in rivalship.[3]

—John Ruskin

9 | Have you been guilty of competing with others?

a | Are you guilty of looking at ministers as competitors?

Dynamic Duel

As you learn to handle specific swords, it is important that you not only know of these weapons but also wield them. Identify an area of conflict in your life specific to harvest and competition. How can you begin to swing this sword of harvest as a *co-laborer*?

Kill or Defend

When environments are changed and paths are cut into former wildernesses, snakes often appear. If we see evil revealed, we do not engage it in our human strength. We slay it with the machete of God's Word: *it is written!*

Harvest is the combination of changing environments and creating paths. Harvesters release the grain in their row while the gatherers collect the produce of their labor. If a predator appears in the field and threatens either the harvest or the harvester, it must be struck down.

Fencing Master

Happy are those who dare courageously to defend what they love.[4]

—Ovid, Roman poet

This job falls to the reaper, not the gatherer, because you cannot fight with full arms.
This means the implement of harvest quickly becomes a tool of defense. Even if a snake is not positioned to strike, it must be beheaded.

Never allow a danger that your labor exposes to slip unchecked or unheralded into the field of another. If you see it, address it. If you are unarmed or not equipped to address it, you must warn others there is a snake in the field.

Sword Play

Find an opportunity for your group to labor for harvest together. Ideas include serving at your local rescue mission, volunteering for a church outreach, or preparing and delivering meals to a family with a new baby.

Room for Reflection

Fencing Lessons

⚜ You are not limited to this earth's light levels.

⚜ What was dangerous in the dark is dealt with in the light.

⚜ God asks us to forge new trails by reopening ancient paths.

⚜ *Ancient* does not mean *old*; it means timeless and eternal.

⚜ Perverse speech leads to perverse ways and crooked paths.

⚜ *Way* is your manner of travel, and *path* is where you're headed.

⚜ You can trail blaze without leaving the path of righteousness.

⚜ Never allow a danger your labor exposes to slip unchecked or unheralded into the field of another.

SKILL CHECK
There is no place for rivals in the Kingdom of God. Each of us journeys along the path of righteousness in her own way.

En Garde

Use God's Word to clear the path, prepare for harvest, and dispatch the enemy.

Impressions

(1) "Myrtle Reed quote," ThinkExist.com, accessed February 15, 2013, http://thinkexist.com/quotation/ if_we_all_tried_to_make_other_people-s_paths_easy/216150.html. (2) Nick Evangelista, *The Inner Game of Fencing: Excellence in Form, Technique, Strategy, and Spirit* (Lincolnwood, IL: Masters Press, 2000), 70. (3) "Rivalry," WorldofQuotes.com, accessed February 15, 2013, http://www.worldofquotes. com/topic/Rivalry/1/index.html. (4) "Ovid quote," BrainyQuote.com, accessed February 15, 2013, http:// www.brainyquote.com/quotes/quotes/o/ovid159362.html.

10

Sword of Light

Returning to the concept of the light saber, *Star Wars* Jedis used their powers of discernment to empower or entrap. Perhaps in the past you had more experience with discernment from the *dark side*. People used it to point out the worst in you (*I can feel your anger*) or used your fears to bind you to themselves.

1 | Have you experienced dark side discernment?

_____

_____

We are not doing that here. We are children of the light. This sword illuminates as it liberates.

> **Our Jesus is the light at the end of a very long and dark tunnel, and when we see Him, we will be like Him.**

Even as a collective Body, our earthbound vantage is dimly lit, limited, and distant. When time is swallowed by eternity, we will see face-to-face in a realm without shadow. Even though we can't see the whole picture, the earth needs us to be discerning and accurate with what we do see.

We all know that we live in a day and time when there is much more than what meets the eye. But living with the wrong focus can overwhelm you. We are charged in Romans 16:19 to "be wise as to what is good and innocent as to what is evil."

2 | How does this verse fit in with what you have experienced as discernment?

_____

_____

_____

3 | Give three New Testament examples of Jesus using discernment to liberate someone He encountered:

_____

_____

_____

_____

G) 4 | In our time, light is distinctly underscored by gross shadow. How might we use this to our advantage?

_____

_____

_____

Throughout the New Testament believers were warned that the earth's last days would yield an environment rife with offense, false teaching, and everything else that breeds deception. Paul described our day to Timothy this way:

*You should know this, Timothy, that in the last days there will be very difficult times. For people will **love only themselves and their money**. They will be **boastful** and **proud**, **scoffing at God**, **disobedient to their parents**, and **ungrateful**. They will consider **nothing sacred**. They will be **unloving** and **unforgiving**; they will **slander others***

*and have **no self-control**. They will be **cruel** and **hate what is good**.*
*They will **betray their friends**, be **reckless**, be **puffed up with pride**,*
*and **love pleasure** rather than God. **They will act religious**,*
*but they will **reject the power that could make them godly**.*
Stay away from people like that!
2 Timothy 3:1–5, NLT

As I read this, I pretty much feel that our current rap artists model these very words.

5 | Music aside, do you believe this accurately describes our time?

_____

_____

a | If Paul felt it was important to warn Timothy about our time back then, how much more do we now need a heightened awareness of our condition in our time?

_____

Notice Paul doesn't say our difficulties are due to economic collapse, bad government, an unstable Middle East, earthquakes, or wars. The condition of the earth, her nations, or their banks is not what strains our time. ***Our struggle arises from a darkened condition of the human heart.***

Throughout the New Testament, we find instructions to *beware, take heed, look to themselves, be on guard, be alert,* and *give careful attention to God's Word and our doctrine.* We are warned against false teachers and the very real danger of self-deception. The worst response to this scenario is to react in fear. Instead of being fearful, let's become experts in what is good. This happens as we study, speak, and live the Word—at home, around the dinner table, and in our relationships.

6 | In 2 Timothy 1:7 we find three tools that help us to combat the spirit of fear that would try to distort our thinking and lead us astray. List these below:

_____

_____

These three qualities empower you to walk in discernment and wield the Word of God appropriately. Without the light of discernment, it is easy to mistake an enemy for a friend and someone's past for their future. This is the very reason we need the sword of the Spirit.

*For the word of God is living and active, sharper than any two-edged sword, piercing to the division of soul and of spirit, of joints and of marrow, and **discerning the thoughts and intentions of the heart**.*
Hebrews 4:12

The very first place this discernment needs to happen is within our own hearts.

7 | Truth time: have you ever mistaken a friend for an enemy or an enemy for a friend?

_____

_____

a | Have you ever thought you were super-spiritual and discerning only to learn later that you were suspicious?

_____

_____

It does us no good if we master the sword only to take it to the throat of an ally. It doesn't matter how strong our legs are if we are holding the wrong ground. It means nothing if our hearts and souls fail where our strength succeeds.

8 | Have you ever woken up and realized you were fighting the wrong battle?

_____

_____

_____

Women and good fencers both have the intuitive ability to see what is coming. But to know what to do with this knowledge, we need heaven's insight so that we are not ignorant of our enemy's devices.

Overcoming Satan's Design

9 | What is Satan's goal? (See page 156.)

_____

_____

_____

_____

a | What tactics does he use to accomplish this?

_____

_____

_____

_____

We counter his attacks with love, power, and a sound mind.

Love

First, love. Listen again to Paul's words:

> _It is my prayer that your love may abound more and more,_
> _with knowledge and all discernment._
> Philippians 1:9

10 | Paul mentions love, knowledge, and discernment. What area did he make the priority?

_____

Fencing Master

Knowledge is love and light and vision.[1]

—Helen Keller

If you have an atmosphere of abounding love, you avoid one _where knowledge puffs up,_ and you make room for _love to build up_ (see 1 Corinthians 8:1). It is my most earnest prayer that this is the atmosphere and motivation for your involvement in this study!

11 | Have you ever experienced the wonder of someone who truly loved discerning the hand of God on your life?

_____

_____

_____

a | What was the fruit of that encounter?

_____

_____

_____

**Hate lives in the dark and therefore
speaks and does dark things.
Love lives in the light and therefore
speaks and does the objective of light.**

Sword Words

Read Philippians 1:9 again. This time, make Paul's prayer your own:
*Father of light, let your love abound more and more in me,
with knowledge and all discernment. Amen.*

Authority and Power
*There is no authority without power, and
no legitimate power without authority.*
[Page 157]

Both our authority and power are found *in Him* and come *from Him*.

*But you are a chosen race, a royal priesthood, a holy nation, a people
for his own possession, that you may proclaim the excellencies of him
who called you out of darkness into his marvelous light.*
1 Peter 2:9

12 | According to this verse, what is the reason we have authority and power?

_____

_____

a | Do we therefore honor God by backing away from our authority or power?

_____

_____

Sound Mind

13 | Define *sound*:

_____

_____

_____

Only God could give us His inward perspective when we are surrounded by a world that is so broken, unhealthy, and diseased in all of its reasoning processes. The Word of God does more than change your mind…it has the power to renew it!

The unsound becomes sound.
The unreasonable becomes reasonable.
The perverse becomes virtuous.
The unbalanced is balanced.
The bipolar becomes centered.
The unstable becomes stable.

14 | What do you need God to do in your mind?

FENCING FACT
You are not a fencer if you do not use your head.[2]

I am not suggesting you stop your medications. They may be what keep you afloat right now, but as I heard one minister say, ultimately they will not get you out of the water. If Jesus could transform a naked, violently dangerous, tomb-roving madman into an ambassador for Him (See Mark 5:1-20), what might He do for you? Dare to begin to believe that God has the gift of a sound mind for you, and do the work to renew it.

Discernment means a diet change. We go from mainly milk to meat.

> *But solid food is for the mature, for those who have their powers of discernment trained by constant practice to distinguish good from evil.*
> Hebrews 5:14

The power of discernment comes with the training of constant use. This is not a once a year or even a once a week practice. As we are in the Word regularly and live the Word brilliantly, we will be constantly using this gift.

15 | Where do you practice discernment?

_____

_____

G) 16 | What does this ability to distinguish good from evil mean?

_____

_____

Seeing More than What Meets the Eye
17 | Fill in the blanks:

Discernment comes with _____, which is ultimately about our _____. (See page 159.)

18 | Is maturity always attached to age?

_____

a | Write down the name of a young woman you know who is discerning.

_____

b | What is it about her that has earned her this designation?

19 | Discernment is *not* about labeling! So what is it about?

Discerning warriors know how to turn evil around for good.

20 | What does this mean?

Discernment can look beyond immediate darkness and distinguish light in the distance. This ability is crucial because we live in a time when people call evil good and good evil and all the lines are blurred.

21 | Give a present example of this distortion and an idea of how we can be light in the distance:

In my opinion, this quote is an excellent example of discernment in action:

Treat people as if they were what they ought to be, and help them to become what they are capable of being.

—Johann Wolfgang von Goethe

22 | Is this how you like to be treated?

a | Is this an example of love believing the best and bringing out the best in others?

Let's do this then! Write down one person you are going to begin treating this way (your husband or children are great places to start):

In this chapter, I shared about my broken sexual past and how my beautiful friends encouraged me. Rather than act as though my past had never happened, they encouraged me to light the tinder of it as a beacon for others. This dynamic of redemption did require time, wisdom, and strategy on my part. I didn't just blurt out the details of my past; I learned how to redeem it. I matured in my new life and left behind the language, ways, and paths of my past.

True discernment understands that the shadowed darkness of one's past can serve as a distant light in someone else's future.
[Page 161]

23 | What are the areas of darkness in your past that might prove to be an awesome bonfire in someone else's future?

Each tree is known by its own fruit. For figs are not gathered from thornbushes, nor are grapes picked from a bramble bush. The good person out of the good treasure of his heart produces good, and the evil person out of his evil treasure produces evil, for out of the abundance of the heart his mouth speaks.
Luke 6:44–45

These verses have proven to be the best guidelines for me. If you are unsure about what a tree is, just wait until the season of fruit. Our landscaper once planted some fruit trees in our yard. I couldn't tell which one was the plum tree and which one was the crab apple tree until it was fruit time; then the evidence was undeniable. In life, it is pretty much the same way. With people, the fruit is their follow-through and their words.

24 | What does it mean to *listen with your heart, then listen to your heart*?

When our hearts are tempered (remember the fire, water, and hammer from chapter seven), we are able to notice what we might have missed before the smog of suspicion was knocked out of us!

Discernment and Prayer

25 | Write down the words that define *intercession*:

> *God never gives us discernment in order that we may criticize, but that we may intercede.*
> —Oswald Chambers

I feel that in the past, we have limited the role of intercession to individuals and prayer. In these dark days, we need to encompass all who carry light. To see this happen, I want to make the following points:

1. Anyone can be an intercessor. It is not an office; it is what all believers can and should do.
2. Intercession can and should happen anywhere.
3. Intercession doesn't always involve prayer. Often it is best expressed through action.
4. Intercessors do not have some kind of special "in" with God; like us, they are in Christ.
5. Intercession should happen whenever light encounters darkness.
6. Intercession should not be weird. It should be as natural as carrying your cross.

Jesus is our greatest example of intercession. Jesus is the ultimate mediator between God and humanity. As He walked the earth, He intervened whenever He encountered the dark forces of sickness, demonic possession, religious distortion, and oppression. He negotiated the religious double-talk of the law experts as He brilliantly arbitrated with astounding wisdom.

> *Fencing Master*
>
> Words which do not give the light of Christ increase the darkness.[3]
>
> —Mother Teresa

Long before Jesus rose from the grave, He rose to every occasion to lift others.

(G) 26 | Give your favorite example of Jesus as an intercessor:

_____

_____

_____

a | Give an example of a time you acted as an intercessor:

_____

_____

Dynamic Duel

What is a stone of judgment you might need to lay aside so you can pick up the sword of light?

_____

_____

_____

Would you get angry if you saw a blind woman stumble and fall? Of course not! Not only would you help her up; you would also walk alongside her so she could safely find her way. In this same way, discernment realizes when others are blind and intercedes (intervenes, arises, mediates, and negotiates) based on their inability and ignorance rather than on their actions. We were blinded by our ignorance and separated from

God by our sins. Jesus did more than discern our situation—He did something about it. He went to the cross to put an end to our plight, and He rose from the dead to give us endless life.

> *Who shall bring any charge against God's elect? It is God who justifies.*
> *Who is to condemn? Christ Jesus is the one who died—more*
> *than that, who was raised—who is at the right hand of God,*
> *who indeed is interceding for us.*
> Romans 8:33–34

27 | What do you think Jesus' current intercession looks like?

_____

_____

_____

Because of Jesus' position of perpetual, risen, and discerning vision we are promised,

> *Who shall separate us from the love of Christ? Shall tribulation, or distress,*
> *or persecution, or famine, or nakedness, or danger, or sword?… No, in all*
> *these things we are more than conquerors through him who loved us.*
> Romans 8:35, 37

Fencing Master

Discernment is God's call to intercession, never to faultfinding.[4]
—Corrie Ten-Boom

Note that it is through *Him who loved us.* It is not *Him who discerned how bad we were* (that was altogether obvious). The very One who knew our worst lit our future. No future dark danger can separate us from Him.

Lovely ones, as we strengthen ourselves in the Word and purify our own hearts, we will be positioned to light this world with true discernment and arise in actions of intercession.

Sword Play

Love is the foundation of true discernment. The following are the seven disciplines of love from 1 Corinthians 13:4-7:

1. Love doesn't react; it is patient and kind.
2. Love doesn't keep a list of past sins.
3. Love trusts God, so it endures.
4. Love celebrates truth.
5. Love doesn't consult the past.
6. Love looks for the best.
7. Love extends itself into the future.

Over the next seven weeks, I want you to work your way down this list. Beginning with *love doesn't react; it is patient and kind,* apply each principle in your everyday life over the course of a week. You can accomplish this by memorizing it, speaking it out loud to keep yourself in check, and most importantly of all, doing it! (A great accountability measure is to involve all your family in the exercise!) Check off each attribute as you go and record the fruit that you saw.

as God's Word
enters our hearts
IT NOT ONLY GUIDES
our soul...
IT ALSO PROVIDES
light.
What is dangerous in the dark
is EXPOSED in the LIGHT

Lisa Bevere
GIRLS WITH SWORDS

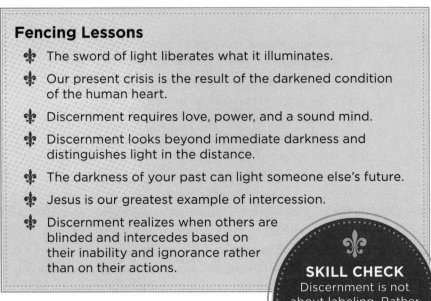

Fencing Lessons

⚜ The sword of light liberates what it illuminates.

⚜ Our present crisis is the result of the darkened condition of the human heart.

⚜ Discernment requires love, power, and a sound mind.

⚜ Discernment looks beyond immediate darkness and distinguishes light in the distance.

⚜ The darkness of your past can light someone else's future.

⚜ Jesus is our greatest example of intercession.

⚜ Discernment realizes when others are blinded and intercedes based on their inability and ignorance rather than on their actions.

SKILL CHECK

Discernment is not about labeling. Rather than dictating "good" or "bad," it acts to turn disadvantage to advantage.

En Garde

I will strengthen myself in the light of true discernment and acts of intercession.

(1) "Light quotes," BrainyQuote.com, accessed February 28, 2013, http://www.brainyquote.com/quotes/keywords/light_3.html. (2) Nick Evangelista, *The Inner Game of Fencing: Excellence in Form, Technique, Strategy, and Spirit* (Lincolnwood, IL: Masters Press, 2000), 11. (3) "Light quotes," BrainyQuote.com, accessed February 28, 2013, http://www.brainyquote.com/quotes/keywords/light.html. (4) "Intercession quotes," oChristian.com, accessed February 27, 2013, http://christian-quotes.ochristian.com/Intercession-Quotes/.

Impressions

11

Sword of Song

Sing and rejoice, O daughter of Zion, for behold, I come and I will dwell in your midst, declares the LORD.
Zechariah 2:10

This chapter is short in this guide but extremely long in application. I wouldn't want the brevity of the pages to cause you to underestimate the power of a song. **Sometimes one song is all it takes to turn the battle in your favor.**

You don't need a worship leader present to lead you into song. You only need to be a daughter, which is a good thing, because there are many battles your Father will lead you into that you will win in song.

So let's review what happens when you worship:
1. The atmosphere is arrested.
2. The very airwaves begin to vibrate and change their pattern.
3. The grip of the enemy is compromised as the friction between dark and light increases.
4. The enemy's movements are slowed.
5. The sounds of accusation are silenced or thrown into confusion.
6. If the vibration of song is intense enough, the enemy withdraws or is disarmed.
7. We leave behind the courts of earth and enter into heaven's.

How amazing is the imagery of the flamberge? The imagery of fire that kept us out is what brings in!

Fencing Master

Praise is the rehearsal of our eternal song.[1]

—Charles Spurgeon

The Word of God declared boldly, as it is sung in adoration and danced to in abandonment before our King, may be the most powerful battle move we can make. My children may not want to see me do this, but my Father loves it! We sing ourselves in, and I believe the angels sing us out!

1 | Have you ever danced alone in worship? How did you feel afterward?

a | Have you ever danced during a worship service? How did you feel during it?

I have been in churches where the worship time was so high-energy I wanted to get up and run around the room! In other services, there was such an atmosphere of quiet reverence I felt ready to rest in His presence. Here's the great news: God can work with both!

> Music improves mood, enhances focus, supports mental health, reduces stress,[2] strengthens the immune system, and promotes rest.[3]

A Song is Born

I want to revisit Moses' song of victory in The Message Bible. (This is one to make you want to run around the room!)

Then Moses and the Israelites sang this song to GOD, giving voice together,

I'm singing my heart out to GOD—what a victory! He pitched horse and rider into the sea. GOD is my strength, GOD is my song, and, yes! GOD is my salvation. This is the kind of God I have and I'm telling the world! This is the God of my father—I'm spreading the news far and wide! GOD is a fighter, pure GOD, through and through....

Your strong right hand, GOD, shimmers with power; your strong right hand shatters the enemy. In your mighty majesty you smash your upstart enemies, you let loose your hot anger and burn them to a crisp. At a blast from your nostrils the waters piled up; tumbling streams dammed up, wild oceans curdled into a swamp....

You blew with all your might and the sea covered them. They sank like a lead weight in the majestic waters. Who compares with you among gods, O GOD? Who compares with you in power, in holy majesty, in awesome praises, wonder-working God?

You stretched out your right hand and the Earth swallowed them up. But the people you redeemed, you led in merciful love; you guided them under your protection to your holy pasture....

...until your people crossed over and entered, O GOD, until the people you made crossed over and entered. You brought them and planted them on the mountain of your heritage, the place where you live, the place you made, your sanctuary, Master, that you established with your own hands. Let GOD rule forever, for eternity!
Exodus 15:1-3, 6-8, 10-13, 16-18

2 | Does this sound like a safe song to you?

_____

Ⓖ   a | Write down a few things this song accomplished:

_____

_____

You can sing whenever or wherever you like! I sing at home, in my car, and in my hotel room. You should begin to collect songs that encourage you, inspire you, and connect you with God's presence!

A Song of Selah

Some songs are better suited to moments of holy reverence. These kinds of songs are usually punctuated with lots of *selahs* (a word Hebrew songwriters used to indicate a time of reflection). David wrote quite a few of these in lieu of flower arranging; they are what brought balance to his warrior side. There are some psalm-type songs that help you truly know that God has felt the anguish of our humanity and has raised us to His lap to comfort us.

Dynamic Duel
What are some practical ways you can weave more of the sword of song into your everyday world?

_____

_____

_____

G Discuss these ideas as a group.

When you sing, not only are you encouraged, God is magnified! As God is magnified His dominion is declared over your situation. When He inhabits the praises of His people, we are before Him even as He is within us. Our hearts begin to swell with His courage as they overflow with gratitude.

Song of Battle

Sword Words

Draw upon Scripture for inspiration—or just pull together some scriptures word for word—and write your own battle song. (You don't have to sing it or write music for it unless you want to.)

_____

_____

_____

_____

Fencing Master

Next to the Word of God, music deserves the highest praise. The gift of language combined with the gift of song was given to man that he should proclaim the Word of God through Music.[4]

—Martin Luther

How you sing is just as important as what you sing. I am not referring to the quality of your voice but to the passion of your approach. There is a time to sing with joy and a time to sing with sadness, but there is never a time to sing disengaged.

3 | According to Isaiah 30:29-32, what can happen when we sing with joy and in unison with instruments?

_____

_____

_____

FENCING FACT

Regardless of what your opponent does, you do what you are supposed to do.[5]

One of the most powerful collections of God's promises is found in Isaiah 54. In this one chapter, we find God's provision of legacy, increase, restoration, redemption, compassion, a sure foundation, freedom from fear, children taught by God, and vindication from the enemy. And you can have it all for a song!

"Sing, O barren one, who did not bear;
break forth into singing and cry aloud,
you who have not been in labor!
For the children of the desolate one will be more
than the children of her who is married," says the LORD.
Isaiah 54:1

As you sing, the very portals of your life open up to heaven's provision.

When I feel tethered, surrounded, limited, or even just earthbound, I pull out my sword of song and lift my voice. Sometimes I put on old songs; others times I put on new ones. For some of you this may mean worshiping with Hillsong United, and for others it may mean Jesus Culture, the Winans, or Southern Gospel. Just sing!

And are you ready to be really daring? Then why not dance as well? Just remember: if you don't want to dance, that's fine, but never despise those who do.

As the ark of the LORD came into the city of David, Michal the daughter of Saul looked out of the window and saw King David leaping and dancing before the LORD, and she despised him in her heart.
2 Samuel 6:16

People are not your audience. God is.

Sword Play

Assemble a collection of powerful truth-songs and, alone or as a group, lift your voice as a worshiping warrior. (It doesn't matter if the songs are live or prerecorded, just that they declare God's Word!) Feel the freedom to dance as you sing!

Room for Reflection

a
SWORD
IS BALANCED
like a tuning instrument
SOMETIMES
ALL IT TAKES IS A
Song
TO TIP THE BATTLE
in your favor

LISA BEVERE
GIRLS WITH SWORDS

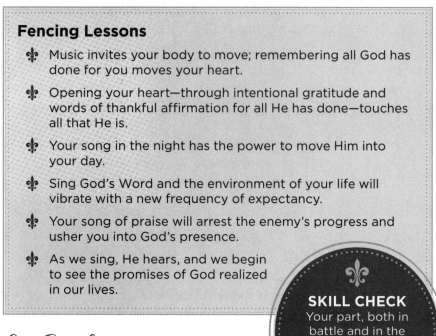

Fencing Lessons

⚜ Music invites your body to move; remembering all God has done for you moves your heart.

⚜ Opening your heart—through intentional gratitude and words of thankful affirmation for all He has done—touches all that He is.

⚜ Your song in the night has the power to move Him into your day.

⚜ Sing God's Word and the environment of your life will vibrate with a new frequency of expectancy.

⚜ Your song of praise will arrest the enemy's progress and usher you into God's presence.

⚜ As we sing, He hears, and we begin to see the promises of God realized in our lives.

SKILL CHECK
Your part, both in battle and in the victory that follows, is to open your mouth and sing His words.

En Garde

God offers a powerful collection of unshakeable promises—and you can have it all for a song!

---

(1) "Praise quotes," oChristian.com, accessed February 28, 2013, http://christian-quotes.ochristian.com/Praise-Quotes/page-4.shtml. (2) "Health benefits of music," NetDoctor, accessed February 28, 2013, http://www.netdoctor.co.uk/healthy-living/wellbeing/health-benefits-of-music.htm. (3) "5 health benefits of music," Yahoo! Health, accessed February 28, 2013, http://health.yahoo.net/experts/allinyourmind/5-health-benefits-music. (4) "Martin Luther quote," Goodreads.com, accessed February 28, 2013, http://www.goodreads.com/quotes/346054-next-to-the-word-of-god-music-deserves-the-highest. (5) Nick Evangelista, *The Inner Game of Fencing: Excellence in Form, Technique, Strategy, and Spirit* (Lincolnwood, IL: Masters Press, 2000), 117.

Impressions

12

Sword of Silence

Our sword of silence is captured in the imagery of a sword that remains within its scabbard. It is present, but contained.

1 | In light of this, what do you think the following quote means?

One sword keeps another in the sheath.
—George Herbert

_____

_____

_____

Silence is a sword unseen because it is a word unspoken or an action untaken.
[Page 175]

Our silence could be likened to a concealed carry license. When a weapon is presented, all the dynamics of a situation change. This sword of silence is carried, yet concealed. When the situation at hand requires that we lay aside all we would—or could—do to tell our side and defend ourselves, then we can choose to lay down, body and soul, at the feet of our King.

2 | Remembering your reading of this chapter, what are some of the things silence can mean?

In addition to what you have listed above, silence can mean *you have a response but have chosen not to give it voice.* This is not about being arrested by fear. It is about responding when God whispers, "Leave this one to me."

3 | Have you ever had Him tell you this? What were the circumstances?

As you probably already know, *remaining still often requires more strength than striking.*

4 | What is the best posture we can assume when we need to hear from God? (See page 176.)

a | Adopting this stance also helps *what* happen for others?

Stilled and silent describes what our present culture calls self-control: "A man without self-control is like a city broken into and left without walls" (Proverbs 25:28).

Our being still and silent (or our inability to do so) reveals if we have rule (or control) of our souls.

5 | How do we find ourselves in the desperate circumstances that require the self-rule of *stilled and silent*? Name two of the causes:

1. _____

_____

2. _____

_____

Let's revisit our example of a "the odds are against you" and "this one is too big for you to handle" battle, the battle between the children of Israel and the Egyptians. God set up what appeared to be an ambush without any means of escape to reveal Himself as the almighty God and Warrior.

Fear not, stand firm, and see the salvation of the Lord, which he will work for you today. For the Egyptians whom you see today, you shall never see again. The Lord will fight for you, and you have only to be silent.
Exodus 14:13–14

6 | What is your favorite promise in these verses?

_____

_____

7 | Do you agree that silence is challenging in moments of terror?

_____

a | What is your normal reaction when you're frightened?

_____

_____

Many times I have nearly choked on what I didn't say—or what I didn't write, or didn't scream. But later I was glad that I swallowed my words.

All would seem clearer if this unseen struggle was as obvious as a real life battle. The battles we face are normally far subtler. The enemy who attacks us is not riding a chariot and throwing spears. Our foe is armed with distorted lies, rumors that twist and isolate, and a fear so intense that it threatens to immobilize. Even so, God's promise stands: that no matter what follows us, He will be our rearguard.

Let's look again at two more versions of these scriptures from Exodus 14. First, from The Message:

> *Moses spoke to the people: "Don't be afraid. Stand firm and watch*
> *God do his work of salvation for you today. Take a good look at the*
> *Egyptians today for you're never going to see them again.*
> *God will fight the battle for you.*
> *And you? You keep your mouths shut!"*
> verses 13-14

And lastly,

> *Moses answered the people, "Do not be afraid. Stand firm and*
> *you will see the deliverance the Lord will bring you today.*
> *The Egyptians you see today you will never see again.*
> *The Lord will fight for you; you need only to be still."*
> verses 13–14, NIV

8 | Which version of this passage is your favorite and why?

_____

_____

_____

9 | What positions us to see the miraculous?

_____

_____

10 | Which is hardest for you?

A. Shutting my mouth

B. Being still

C. Standing my ground

D. All of the above

11 | What does it mean to "stand firm" or "hold your ground"?

_____

_____

_____

_____

_____

_____

_____

> YOU MAY HAVE >>>>>>>>>>>>
> private battles of your own.
> YOU MAY HAVE <<<<<<<<<<<<
> won victories no one knew
> how to celebrate...
> BE PATIENT..............
> GOD never wastes a
> ⇒➔ private victory.
> there is a day on earth
> or in heaven when
> THE victory WILL BE
> celebrated!
> Lisa Bevere
> GIRLS WITH SWORDS

12 | Why did God deliberately and repeatedly harden Pharaoh's heart?

_____

_____

Later, we see that King Hezekiah followed Moses' lead when he lifted up a prayer that we would all do well to make our own.

> _So now, O LORD our God, save us from his hand, that all the kingdoms of the earth may know that you alone are the LORD._
> Isaiah 37:20

The battles we face personally, in our families, as a nation, and even as Christians are so much larger than any of us have the capacity to realize this side of eternity. A battle is never a showdown between nations, religions, or individuals; it is always another opportunity for a revelation of the one true God.

Look how God answered King Hezekiah's prayer:

> _Behold, I will put a spirit in him, so that he shall hear a rumor and return to his own land, and I will make him fall by the sword in his own land._
> Isaiah 37:7

The one who openly threatened God's people was defeated by a cloaked rumor. This should serve as a warning to all of us that chasing a rumor can prove deadly.

Speech is silver; silence is golden.
—Ancient Egyptian proverb

13 | I loved seeing both sides of this famous saying. What do you think this quote means?

_____

_____

_____

Individual Struggles

There are times in life when the battle is *very* personal! Are you in the midst of a personal challenge now?

_____

_____

_____

I have already been honest in saying that the sword of silence is the most difficult one for me to carry. I also know that I must learn to carry it better with each passing day. I find it *very* hard to be quiet when I am misunderstood (and therefore misrepresented).

14 | What is the area you find the most difficult to be silent in?

⚔ *Fencing Master*

It is more noble by silence to avoid an injury than by argument to overcome it.[1]

—Francis Beaumont

_____

_____

_____

The book of Proverbs promises us, "Fire goes out without wood, and quarrels disappear when gossip stops" (26:20, NLT).

(G) 15 | What are some ways to put out this fire?

_____

_____

16 | Our tongue has the power of which two extremes? (See Proverbs 18:21)

_____

Dynamic Duel

After reading the story of mine and John's personal battle, did you realize that you've muddied some waters?

_____

What can you do now?

_____

_____

_____

Sometimes allowing a stream of silence to follow the muddy river of self-defense is your only option. When the time is right for speaking again, you will know.

David's Sword of Silence

17 | Have you ever felt like David, ready to snap after a long streak of faithfulness because you were not included in something?

_____

_____

_____

If you are not careful, listening to what other people say about you may cause you to forget who you actually are.

The importance of this point cannot be overstated. In our current day and age of social media, you must constantly allow God's Word to be the only framework that defines you. You are not defined by the number of followers you have on Twitter, the likes on your Instagram, or how many friend requests are on your Facebook. The only one who counts is the One who will stick closer than a brother. Far too many have been bullied into conforming or compromising for the sake of being included; even worse, others have actually killed themselves because they couldn't take the rejection they faced. Remember, we are in *Him*!

Fencing Master

Some of the greatest battles will be fought within the silent chambers of your own soul.[2]

—Ezra Taft Benson

You can allow criticism to refine you, but *never* allow it to define you! Like David, you must know what you are anointed to *do* and not be distracted from your purpose. Nabal was a fool, but David was so road weary he must have believed him to be a valid source of affirmation. Likewise, the enemy will send fools across your path.

18 | What is the message that fools bring, and why do they bring it?

The following are key takeaway points from David's encounter with a fool. Circle the ones that speak to you.

1. God alone establishes houses.
2. When we live under the directive of God's Spirit, God protects us.
3. God knows how to settle matters with our enemies.
4. We should never use our position with God to protect ourselves.
5. We are not to take matters of judgment or salvation into our own hands; both of these belong to our God.

Silence is the element in which great things fashion themselves together; that at length they may emerge, full-formed and majestic, into the daylight of Life, which they are thenceforth to rule.

—Thomas Carlyle

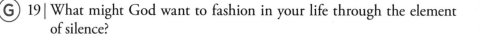

(G) 19 | What might God want to fashion in your life through the element of silence?

_____

_____

_____

A New Kind of Weapon

Lovely mothers, sisters, daughters, and friends, chances are someone has insulted you. Maybe your name has been paired with insinuating accusations. Is there an invitation that never finds its way to your door? Please believe me, I understand. But are you truly willing to allow an insult or oversight to derail or sabotage your destiny? You long to strike, but the sword you now hold that you thought was anointed is actually called vengeance, and it is not yours to wield. Resheath your sword and lay it down!

Are you upset because you are riding alongside someone else who has been maligned and dishonored? Dismount immediately, remind her of God's promises, and tell her to stand still and watch God, our rear guard, take over. My friend, God will establish your house and watch over you as you go forth. You don't have to figure out what needs to happen to those you per-ceive to be enemies. God has it all sorted out; rest in the knowledge that he alone is the righteous judge. It is time we move away from postures of self-protection. God fights for us as we fight on behalf of others.

FENCING FACT

In fencing, pointless action wastes your energy and gives your opponent the advantage.[3]

Take up a different kind of weapon—a sword called silence.
[Page 187]

Jesus is our ultimate example in the mastery of silence. He wasn't quiet because there was nothing He could say. He wasn't still because there was nothing He could do. He was lifted up from the ground so that in Him, we could hold ours.

Jesus spoke the loudest in his silence, **and it is time we likewise recognize when it is right to remain silent.**

All we like sheep have gone astray; we have turned—every one—to his own way; and the Lord has laid on him the iniquity of us all.
He was oppressed, and he was afflicted, yet he opened not his mouth; like a lamb that is led to the slaughter, and like a sheep that before its shearers is silent, so he opened not his mouth.
Isaiah 53:6–7

In the story of human existence, all of us have strayed, turned, and gone our own ways. But this is not about our past; this is about our future. God is asking us to be part of the end of this story—the part in which we do things His way.

Jesus spoke the loudest in his silence. There was no need for words of earth to be voiced when the word of heaven stood before them, silent, as they condemned themselves so that through him all would be saved.
[Page 189]

20 | What battle needs to be won through your silence?

_____

_____

_____

_____

Sword Words

When he was reviled, he did not revile in return;
when he suffered, he did not threaten, but continued
entrusting himself to him who judges justly.
1 Peter 2:23

Are you ready to entrust your life to the just Judge? Write and declare a prayer telling Him so.

_____

_____

_____

You can do this! He has already gone before us and made a way; all we must do is follow!

Sword Play

Wielding silence as a weapon is anything but passive. It requires intentional choice to guard your mouth and put your trust in God. As a group, discuss actions you can take to respond in silent faith (e.g., walking away from a conversation or responding to someone by text message to guard your words).

Room for Reflection

_____

_____

_____

_____

_____

_____

Fencing Master

Courage is not simply one of the virtues, but the form of every virtue at the testing point.[4]

—C. S. Lewis

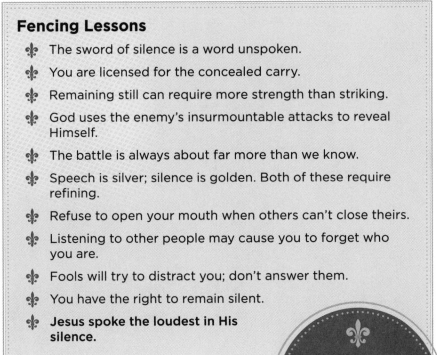

Fencing Lessons

- ✤ The sword of silence is a word unspoken.
- ✤ You are licensed for the concealed carry.
- ✤ Remaining still can require more strength than striking.
- ✤ God uses the enemy's insurmountable attacks to reveal Himself.
- ✤ The battle is always about far more than we know.
- ✤ Speech is silver; silence is golden. Both of these require refining.
- ✤ Refuse to open your mouth when others can't close theirs.
- ✤ Listening to other people may cause you to forget who you are.
- ✤ Fools will try to distract you; don't answer them.
- ✤ You have the right to remain silent.
- ✤ **Jesus spoke the loudest in His silence.**

SKILL CHECK
God has it all sorted out. We can be silent before our accusers, just as Jesus was, and allow our Father to defend us.

En Garde
Trusting God in the face of threats and insults is a constant process.

(1) "Francis Beaumont quote," QuotationsBook.com, accessed March 4, 2013, http://quotationsbook.com/quote/36196/. (2) "Ezra Taft Benson quote," ThinkExist.com, accessed March 4, 2013, http://thinkexist.com/quotation/some_of_the_greatest_battles_will_be_fought/204550.html. (3) Nick Evangelista, *The Inner Game of Fencing: Excellence in Form, Technique, Strategy, and Spirit* (Lincolnwood, IL: Masters Press, 2000), 97. (4) "C.S. Lewis quote," QuotationsBook.com, accessed March 13, 2013, http://quotationsbook.com/quote/8773/.

Impressions

13

Sword of Forgiveness and Restoration

This sword differs from the last one we discussed, the sword of silence, in that it is no longer carried—it is laid aside. This laying aside is described as an act of *fealty*. We are not just yielding our words; we are letting go of the sword.

This time envision a sword resting at the foot of a throne. The sword is yielded for a moment so that later it may be wielded for a greater purpose.

Can you see this?

It is one thing to have a sword and refuse to draw it, and quite another to have no sword at all.

Our approach in this chapter will be very different from the previous chapters. This will not be a chapter where I will write and you will fill in the blanks; this is a chapter you will write. This is where the lack of any weapon will reveal your motives.

> ⚔ *Fencing Master*
>
> Forgiveness is an act of the will, and the will can function regardless of the temperature of the heart.[1]
>
> —Corrie ten Boom

1 | List some of the dirty, human weapons mentioned in Galatians: (See page 192.)

_____

_____

_____

2 | In contrast to what you listed above, for what reason have we been empowered?

_____

_____

Fencing Master

Without forgiveness, there's no future.[2]

—Desmond Tutu

I have been very honest and open about my struggles with my father:

The phone never rang, but I did hear the voice of my Father. My heavenly one whispered a question into my spirit: "Lisa, do you know I love your father more than you love your father?"

In all honesty at the time I found this revelation a bit shocking, so I remained quiet. The whisper continued, "I want him with me more than you want him with me. Lisa, give him to me... You can't save him."

[Pages 194-195]

After reading the account of my father's story, think about your own.

3 | Who is it that you are trying to get saved so your life might be easier or your testimony more valid?

_____

_____

4 | Do you know that God loves those we perceive to be enemies in our households or to our faith?

_____

_____

_____

_____

I don't want to scare you, but God loves the unlovely and the unloving. He does not love or approve of what they do, but (just as He did with us) in Christ, He loved them *before*.

I believe God loved my father long *before* he became an alcoholic. He knew my father when he was a frightened immigrant boy whose father and sister had died. I have every reason to believe that my father prayed when they were starving and penniless. He would have prayed when my grandmother's next husband beat him. He would have cried out when he ran away from home. I couldn't see these things because I did not know my father before he was my father—but God did.

> ## *Fencing Master*
> A person who cannot forgive has forgotten how great a debt God has forgiven them.[3]
>
> —John Bevere

Maybe this will help you understand that God loved your abuser *before* something dark came in and twisted their soul, before they did the unthinkable and unspeakable to you.

He loved that mother *before* you knew her, when she was a little girl who nobody protected and nobody wanted. He heard her cry out when she thought no one heard. When she had you, she didn't know how to be a mother, because no one had ever mothered her *before*.

That was *before*, and here we stand *now*.

Our King is asking us to forgive them just as we were forgiven. He first loved us *before* so we can now love them. God wants you to let Him be a door into your house.

Sword Words

*Believe on the Lord Jesus Christ, and thou
shalt be saved, and thy house.*
Acts 16:31, KJV

Who do you need to entrust to this faithful promise of God?

This is His promise. You don't want to shut the door on it. Believe it, and don't be afraid (or, as in my case, stop being weird). Just love them.

I am not asking you to be foolish. Don't leave your children alone with someone who *before* was abusive or perverse, and don't move back in with a man who beats you; but now is the time to forgive them!

Faith is the deliberate confidence in the character of God whose ways you may not understand at the time.
—Oswald Chambers

Our faith is placed in God, not in people.

5 | Have you asked the questions I asked?
   Why didn't my father or mother love me?
   Why don't they want to be with my children?
   When will Your promise come true?

Have you ever felt orphaned? Then you need to know that His whisper to me is His promise to you as well:

"You are looking at this all wrong. What you see as rejection I see as adoption.... When you are completely abandoned by your natural father, you are utterly adopted by me. In a sense your father has renounced any claim he had to you and your children. Now nothing stands between us. You are all mine."
[Page 197]

If God is, in fact, a Father to the fatherless, then we are suddenly no longer fatherless. We are fathered! He adopted us long before we were abandoned. **Before anyone else knew how to love you, He said, "I want her!"**

Look at God's warning to people who might consider exploiting or abusing the vulnerable:

*You must not exploit a widow or an orphan. If you exploit them in any way and they cry out to me, then I will certainly hear their cry. My anger will blaze against you, and I will kill you with the **sword**. Then your wives will be widows and your children fatherless.*
Exodus 22:22-24, NLT

Fencing Master

To love means loving the unlovable. To forgive means pardoning the unpardonable. Faith means believing the unbelievable. Hope means hoping when everything seems hopeless.[4]

—G.K. Chesterton

This has never been a light matter to Him!
But He alone is the Judge of all. He alone has the right to have anger that blazes. We cry and He hears! In Psalm 68:5, He promises to be a Father to the fatherless. There is no reason we should doubt, no reason we should look to our fathers to be what only God can ultimately be.

6 | Maybe your issue is not with a father. Maybe it is with a mother, a sister, a brother, or even a husband or child. Who is it you are afraid to love?

a | What might God be asking you to say to them?

_____

_____

_____

_____

_____

7 | Who might be waiting for you to be a living example of this:

If you forgive the sins of any, they are forgiven them; if you withhold forgiveness from any, it is withheld.

John 20:23

_____

_____

_____

FENCING FACT
The art of fencing is in the control of behavior and movement.[5]

What's Your Story?

Now, lovely one, how about you? I don't know your story, but I can tell you without question that God is faithful.

8 | Are there any daggers of disappointment or bitterness that might threaten to misdirect the sword in your hand?

_____

_____

_____

_____

_____

The truth is, I still judged my father until the moment I spoke the words God gave me. When I released him, I was released. Our King has a way of healing both parties through the actions of one.

Deep wounds that remain unhealed can cause us to lash out and injure the very ones heaven longs to heal. The King has conquered your heart; now He wants to use your life for His purpose of restoration.

There is no revenge so complete as forgiveness.
—Josh Billings

G 9 | What does this mean?

_____

_____

_____

Will you be brave enough to lay aside the daggers of rejection and disappointment? Will you allow our Father to remake them into instruments of adoption, restoration, and divine appointment?

10 | How might God want to use you as an agent of restoration?

_____

_____

_____

_____

11 | Where can the King send you to speak the words others need to hear so that they can receive His healing and life?

_____

_____

_____

_____

Will you speak His counsel rather than rehearse your hurts?

G 12 | How might you bless someone who has hurt you?

_____

_____

_____

I am not asking you to repeat my words, but I am asking you to speak our Father's words into situations and individuals that are crying out to be restored. I know you wish it had all been different. I understand. You didn't write the beginning of your story, but you can choose to let God write the ending. *Love never fails.*

Fencing Master

People are often unreasonable and self-centered. Forgive them anyway.[6]

—Mother Teresa

Sword Play

Write a small version of your forgiveness story below. Be sure to include the ending.

Fencing Lessons

⚜ God loves the enemies in our households and of our faith.

⚜ God does not love or approve of what these people do, but (just as He did with us) in Christ, He loved them *before*.

⚜ Our King asks us to forgive just as we were forgiven.

⚜ God loved us *before* so that we can *now* love them.

⚜ God wants you to open the door to your house for Him.

⚜ God calls the *wrong* of mankind's rejection His *rights* to your adoption.

⚜ God adopted you before you were abandoned.

⚜ You may have had a horrible beginning, but with God, you can choose your ending.

SKILL CHECK

It is important to discover if you are fighting against someone or rather fighting on their behalf.

En Garde

Speak our Father's words to those who are crying out to be restored.

I DON'T *know* YOUR *Story* *but I can tell you* & GOD IS *faithful*

LISA BEVERE *girls* WITH *Swords*

Impressions

(1) "Quotes about Forgiveness," Goodreads.com, accessed March 1, 2013, http://www.goodreads.com/quotes/tag?utf8=%E2%9C%93&id=forgiveness. (2) "Desmond Tutu quote," BrainyQuote.com, accessed March 4, 2013, http://www.brainyquote.com/quotes/quotes/d/desmondtut379846.html. (3) John Bevere, *The Bait of Satan: Living Free from the Deadly Trap of Offense* (Lake Mary, FL: Charisma House, 2004), 120. (4) "G.K. Chesterton quote," QuotationsBook.com, accessed March 5, 2013, http://quotationsbook.com/quote/19424/. (5) Nick Evangelista, The Art and Science of Fencing (Lincolnwood, IL: Masters Press, 1996), 81. (6) "Mother Teresa quote," Goodreads.com, accessed March 1, 2013, http://www.goodreads.com/quotes/6396-people-are-often-unreasonable-and-self-centered-forgive-them-anyway-if.

Christina's Dream

I recently received the story of another dream. In it, a young woman found herself near the edge of a forest, when suddenly, she spotted a lion. Most of us would run in fear, but instead, the girl stayed where she was, thinking, *I'll be fine. I have a sword lying beside me.*

As the lion drew nearer, she called out for help, but no one responded. She stood, trembling, and lifted her weapon only to realize it was too heavy.

Panicked, she swung her the sword at the lion's neck. She struck with the flat of the blade. The blow was utterly ineffective; her sword clattered to the ground, and she woke in a panic.

Two things stand out to me: first, this young woman had underestimated the size of her adversary. Second, even though she possessed a sword, she did not have the strength or skill to wield it. My sisters, allow this dream to serve as an admonition—so that neither of these would be true of us.

Cross Carry

As you now know, we possess both a cross and a crown. For the most part the cross we carry is invisible. We see its effect but not its form. Likewise, in Christ we have been given an invisible crown.

> *What is man, that you are mindful of him, or the son of man,*
> *that you care for him? You made him for a little while lower*
> *than the angels; you have crowned him with glory and honor,*
> *putting everything in subjection under his feet.*
>
> Hebrews 2:6–8

Jesus is crowned with glory and honor, and everything is subject to Him. This means that in Christ, we have authority over darkness. On the earth, the crown we wear represents our position of authority.

Fencing Master

You're not likely to err by practicing too much of the cross.[1]

—John Bunyan

I recently received a story that underscores just how crucial it is that we walk in our authority in Christ. It came from a caring mother of four who openly shared that her beautiful, intelligent six-year-old daughter was in an ongoing struggle with some very dark and persistent thoughts. Listen to this mother's words…

She started saying she hated herself, didn't want to live. When asked what she wanted to be when she was older, she would reply, "I just want to die." I know kids go through moments of this to shock or try to get what they want. But this was different and disturbing and dark.

As time went on, the statements and melancholy were increasing. It absolutely broke my heart. Childhood should be fun and joyful, and she was being robbed. It was horrible for the "now," but horrific when I thought about the future. I felt so guilty; where had I messed up in my parenting?

I spoke to only a few close people about it. I didn't want my precious girl judged or excluded by other Christian families. My mum committed it to the Lord, my husband thought she needed more discipline, my close friend thought she needed a child psychologist. I prayed anxious, tearful, worried prayers.

But I still felt helpless. My prayers were going unanswered. It hung over me like an oppressive cloud. Whenever I was at church, it would hit me the worst. By the time the women's conference came, I was being tormented by it. I was desperate for help. Then on Saturday you spoke about spiritual authority (our crown), not praying anxious prayers—but as His daughters, in His household, with His given authority because of Christ in us, we have authority against ALL the powers and principalities that come against us.

Well, when I got home that night I woke up my husband. "We need to pray with authority now!" So we did. Then I felt to go and pray over her. Bit tricky when you are trying not to wake her or her younger, sleepy sister, but as quietly as possible I went after the devil in Jesus' name.

When I finished praying, she woke up and smiled at me. I knew from the moment I had finished praying over her that something had lifted and the burden I was carrying was no longer there. It was awesome.

There was an instant change in her behavior, but the best came a few days later when she told me about a dream she had. She told me Jesus came down to her and hugged her, and she felt God's love and peace all around her. When I asked her when she had that dream, she replied it was Saturday night. I'm pretty confident to say it was after she was prayed for.

Do you see what can happen when we wake up, as we are charged to do?

We must wake ourselves up! Or somebody else will take our place, and bear our cross, and thereby rob us of our crown.
—William Booth

Both the cross you carry and the crown you wear are personal. This amazing, caring, concerned mother remembered that she wore a crown.

This testimony just came to me yesterday, but I remember this meeting. I had intended to preach on one subject and felt I should put away my notes and speak as a mother to the mothers. This mother did not need me to pray for her daughter; there was no one better suited to pray over the daughter than her mother. What I did was remind her of who she is in Christ.

But just as we stated when we opened this book, we must not pray the problem. We must pray the answer with confident expectancy. We approach His throne as confident warrior daughters who know who they are in Christ and what they carry upon their lives.

Learn to know Christ and him crucified. Learn to sing to him, and say, "Lord Jesus, you are my righteousness, I am your sin. You have taken upon yourself what is mine and given me what is yours. You have become what you were not so that I might become what I was not."
—Martin Luther

We wear the crown, and we carry the cross. Jesus bore our cross so we could wear His crown. He became like us. Isn't it time we became like Him? This dynamic of becoming like Christ is realized through discipleship, which we live by daily walking with Him.

Then Jesus told his disciples, "If anyone would come after me,
let him deny himself and take up his cross and follow me."
Matthew 16:24

1 | How do we fulfill this highly personalized directive?

_____

_____

_____

_____

The Cross is personal.

2 | What are the three elemental instructions of Matthew 16:24?

_____

_____

_____

G) 3 | What makes the cross personal?

_____

_____

_____

_____

I have no doubt that, truly, the cross captures *all that the work of salvation* has placed in our hands.

4 | On this page I want you to answer, what has it personally meant to you?

_____

_____

_____

_____

The cross is far from an ornament to wear; it is an order to carry out.

5 | Can you identify with my lack of clarity on what it means to "carry my cross"?

I love how the very moment we admit our need, God is there to meet it.

6 | In what area can you admit need right now?

When I admitted my need for insight and wisdom, God sent me to retrieve what I had already collected. When I had organized and clearly outlined all that I knew, He added in His words:

"Behold the Cross. All of these words and more represent the Cross. Carry these with you into your everyday world."

The Cross provides all that it won, just as Jesus provides all that He is!

[Page 212]

I have added the word *weapon* to the collection of words that were so generously provided. Are there any words you'd like to add?

Do you see how simply Paul put this? Contained within us is an unlimited, immeasurable, precious treasure.

> *We carry this precious Message [of the Cross] around in the*
> *unadorned clay pots of our ordinary lives.*
> 2 Corinthians 4:7, The Message

As containers, we should not filter the gospel. We simply carry it with us, and when the need arises, we pour it out. We have the ability to carry the cross everywhere that life takes us.

I want you to pretend God is speaking directly to you through Paul's words:

So brave Daughter,

Here's what I want you to do, God helping you: Take your everyday, ordinary life—your sleeping, eating, going-to-work, and walking-around life—and place it before God as an offering. Embracing what God does for you is the best thing you can do for him. Don't become so well-adjusted to your culture that you fit into it without even thinking. Instead, fix your attention on God. You'll be changed from the inside out. Readily recognize what he wants from you, and quickly respond to it. (Romans 12:1–2, MSG)

Most lovingly,
Your Father

Even though I travel and minister, Jesus still needs my everyday, ordinary life. Every waking moment of His life was a message; why shouldn't ours be the same? Consider making a personalized version of this directive part of your daily prayer:

> *"Heavenly Father, may **everything** that the crucifixion of Your Son provided gain **full expression in and through my life today**. I choose to deny sin and my former limitations as I magnify Your work and follow You."*

> It is time our world saw Jesus lifted up
> and Christ in us the hope of glory.

Our Cross-Carry

7 | Let's walk through this together. Do we all agree that the cross was God's ultimate display of His unconditional love?

a | As you read the Gospels, how do you see Jesus loving people?

Jesus spoke truth, fed the hungry, cast out demons, healed the sick, confronted religion, and raised the dead. Not bad for an everyday, ordinary life. The following scriptures are ways we can *follow Him*.

> *And he went throughout all Galilee, teaching in their synagogues*
> *and* proclaiming the gospel of the kingdom *and* healing
> every disease and every affliction *among the people.*
> Matthew 4:23

And,

> *[Jesus said,] "Take heart, my son; your sins are forgiven." And behold,*
> *some of the scribes said to themselves, "This man is blaspheming."*
> *But Jesus, knowing their thoughts, said, "Why do you think evil in*
> *your hearts? For which is easier, to say, 'Your sins are forgiven,' or to say,*
> *'Rise and walk'?* But that you may know that the Son of Man has
> authority on earth to forgive sins"—*he then said to the paralytic—*
> "Rise, pick up your bed and go home." *And he rose and went home.*
> *When the crowds saw it, they were afraid, and they glorified God,*
> *who had given such authority to men.*
> Matthew 9:2–8

And finally,

> *God anointed Jesus of Nazareth with the Holy Spirit and*
> *with power. He went about doing good and healing all who*
> *were oppressed by the devil, for God was with him.*
> Acts 10:38

> *And when they saw him they worshiped him, but some doubted.*
> *And Jesus came and said to them, "All authority in heaven and on earth*
> *has been given to me. Go therefore and make disciples of all nations,*
> *baptizing them in the name of the Father and of the Son and of the*
> *Holy Spirit, teaching them to observe all that I have commanded you.*
> *And behold, I am with you always, to the end of the age."*
> Matthew 28:17–20

There is no reason to choose between social justice and the supernatural. Jesus did both. Let's remove our name from the equation, call him Emanuel—"God with us"—and do the same.

Redemption

FENCING FACT

You aren't a good fencer because you win. You win because you are a good fencer.[2]

The word *redemption* has a massive reach, and by definition it includes salvation, exchange, deliverance, rescue, refurbishment, restoration, and recovery. You can express the cross that purchased redemption to others through your daily life.

> *Let the redeemed of the LORD say so,*
> *whom he has redeemed from trouble.*
> Psalm 107:2

Here are some of the troubles Psalm 107 says God's people had gotten into:
[ ] Wandering in desert wastes
[ ] Hunger and thirst
[ ] Faintness of soul
[ ] Sitting in darkness and the shadow of death
[ ] Imprisonment in affliction and irons
[ ] Rebelling against the word of God

[ ] Spurning the counsel of the Most High
[ ] Becoming foolish through their sinful ways
[ ] Suffering affliction because of iniquity
[ ] Drawing near to the gates of death
[ ] Losing their courage on stormy seas
[ ] Coming to their wits' end
[ ] Being diminished and brought low through oppression, evil, and sorrow

Know this, whether you've messed up or found yourself in a mess at no fault of your own, *God redeems*. Regardless of how we got into a place of trouble, He leads us out and into His place of goodness. He alone has the power to save, and we who have been redeemed should say so! This is another way we carry our crosses. To be practical in our application, I would love to see you *check off* all the items on the list that apply to you.

What emblem has the power to proclaim the gospel of the Kingdom better than the cross? Did Christ's sacrifice through the cross heal your life, body, and relationships? Do you believe it still has the power to heal every disease and affliction? **We know that Jesus is the same yesterday, today, and forever. Can't the same be said of the cross?**

If He is with us and He is the same, then He is willing to display on earth all that the cross has purchased.

Afterward he appeared to the eleven themselves as they were reclining at table, and he rebuked them for their unbelief and hardness of heart, because they had not believed those who saw him after he had risen. And he said to them, "Go into all the world and proclaim the gospel to the whole creation. Whoever believes and is baptized will be saved, but whoever does not believe will be condemned. And these signs will accompany those who believe: in my name they will cast out demons; they will speak in new tongues; they will pick up serpents with their hands; and if they drink any deadly poison, it will not hurt them; they will lay their hands on the sick, and they will recover."
Mark 16:14–18

8 | List the areas that Jesus had to address in order that His disciples (including us) could follow Him and see signs and wonders.

We don't need to chase after demons, but if you follow Jesus long enough, you will probably encounter them.

(G) 9 | Is this uncomfortable for you?

a | Have you already seen people set free or an atmosphere shifted from oppressive to free?

It doesn't matter if you have or have not seen this yet. Don't let this be different than any other area you would encounter in your everyday, ordinary world. Use the sword of God's Word to silence demons, and then cast them out in Jesus' name.

If you speak in tongues, speak in tongues. It will build up your holy faith. If you don't speak in tongues, speak heaven's truth in whatever language you have access to.

Fencing Master

All heaven is interested in the cross of Christ, all hell is terribly afraid of it, while men are the only beings who more or less ignore its meaning.[3]

—Oswald Chambers

Jesus promised that as we touched the sick, recovery would happen. You may say, "Well, that was only for the time immediately after His resurrection." I remember reading that when Mother Teresa chose to come into contact with the lepers, the treatment that stopped the spread of this highly infectious disease was discovered.[4] It would seem God had scientists do what they could—in order that Mother Teresa could be the hands of Jesus and be about God's business!

10 | Who or what is God asking you to touch so that He might get involved?

_____

_____

_____

_____

_____

*Now many signs and wonders were **regularly** done among the people by the hands of the apostles. And they were all together in Solomon's Portico.*
Acts 5:12

*And **every day**, in the temple and from house to house, they did not cease teaching and preaching that the Christ is Jesus.*
verse 42

I am desperate to see signs, wonders, teaching, and preaching as part of everyone's everyday. I truly believe we can see this happen if we behave like the early Church. They took the living, breathing, life-transforming message of the cross everywhere they went. As they went through their daily lives, hearts were encouraged, the sick were healed, and the oppressed were set free. Why shouldn't the same be true of us?

Are you looking for a sign that Jesus still wants to do wonders? The cross is our sign, and you are His wonder!

A minimalistic gospel produces minimal results. Preaching half the benefits of the cross produces half the cross's benefits. None of this should surprise us. Diluted derivatives should never be expected to produce the results of full strength. As we speak the Word in the fullness of its strength, we will be strengthened in the fullness of life. We will see for ourselves the true effects of life more abundant.

My speech and my preaching was not with enticing words of man's wisdom, but in demonstration of the Spirit and of power: That your faith should not stand in the wisdom of men, but in the power of God.
1 Corinthians 2:4–5, KJV

Preaching a powerful gospel produces powerful results.

11 | What results do you hope to see in your life and family?

_____

_____

_____

a | In your church and community?

_____

_____

_____

Sword Words

What are you willing to speak and preach to see this fruit in your world?

_____

_____

_____

Living Swords

Lovely one, I am so honored that you have chosen to delve deeper and taken the time to sharpen your sword and shoulder your cross. It is time we, the hope-filled prisoners of the earth, become the worshiping daughters of Judah—those likened to a bow our God will pull to shoot the arrows of Ephraim into the future. It is time we extend His reach, allowing our lives to strike at the darkness like a sword in His hand.

Come home, hope-filled prisoners!
This very day I'm declaring a double bonus—
everything you lost returned twice-over!
***Judah is now my weapon**, the bow I'll pull,*
*setting **Ephraim as an arrow** to the string.*
I'll wake up your sons, O Zion,
to counter your sons, O Greece.
From now on
people are my swords.
Zechariah 9:12–13, The Message

Just as Jesus was the Word of the Father made flesh, our lives are to become the Word of Jesus made flesh. Because the Word of God is the sword of the Spirit and Jesus was the Word made flesh, as His body we too become living swords.

He makes his messengers winds, his ministers a flaming fire.
Psalm 104:4

We are flaming swords who proclaim He is the way.

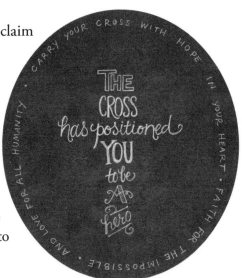

The Cross positioned you to be
a hero.
Carry it with hope in your
heart,
faith for the impossible,
and love for all humanity.

The disciples didn't have the length of days or even the room to record all the things Jesus did.

Now there are also many other things that Jesus did.
Were every one of them to be written, I suppose that the world
itself could not contain the books that would be written.
John 21:25

You are His chosen and living expression of wonder. Become one with Him, just as He is one with the Father. As you do, our broken world will glimpse His bride rising in His stature, and many will be won.

> *Chosen Daughter of God,*
> *Turn from your reflection,*
> *deny its limitations, and reflect Him.*
> *Remember daily His faithfulness in your past*
> *because it will be your strength in your future.*
> *Develop your ability to listen to the Holy Spirit.*
> *Draw near to God and He will draw so very near to you.*
> *Recite your verses with bold confidence.*
> *Lay hold of the cross and live with daily acts of heroism.*
> *Target the enemy and strike sure.*

I am so honored to be walking the earth alongside you, shoulder to shoulder with our crosses held high as we follow our glorious King into His eternal realm.

God hold us to that which drew us first, when the Cross was the attraction, and we wanted nothing else.[5]
—Amy Wilson-Carmichael

Sword Play

Now that you have glimpsed the breadth and beauty of what it means to carry your cross—live it! Wherever you see the opportunity to carry the gospel of the Kingdom in your everyday, ordinary life, do so with bold strength!

Room for Reflection

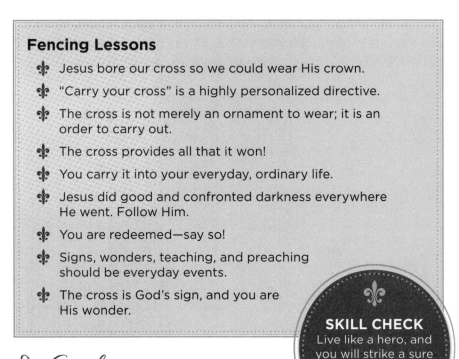

Fencing Lessons

⚜ Jesus bore our cross so we could wear His crown.

⚜ "Carry your cross" is a highly personalized directive.

⚜ The cross is not merely an ornament to wear; it is an order to carry out.

⚜ The cross provides all that it won!

⚜ You carry it into your everyday, ordinary life.

⚜ Jesus did good and confronted darkness everywhere He went. Follow Him.

⚜ You are redeemed—say so!

⚜ Signs, wonders, teaching, and preaching should be everyday events.

⚜ The cross is God's sign, and you are His wonder.

SKILL CHECK
Live like a hero, and you will strike a sure blow to the enemy, and captives will be set free.

En Garde
No longer think of yourself as *targeted*. You were first *chosen* to be a sword lifted in our Savior's hand.

(1) "Quotes about the cross," Goodreads.com, accessed March 1, 2013, http://www.goodreads.com/quotes/tag?id=cross&page=2&utf8=%E2%9C%93. (2) Nick Evangelista, *The Inner Game of Fencing: Excellence in Form, Technique, Strategy, and Spirit* (Lincolnwood, IL: Masters Press, 2000), 56. (3) "Cross of Christ," Sermon Index, accessed March 4, 2013, http://www.sermonindex.net/modules/articles/index.php?view=article&aid=13819. (4) David Van Biema, *Mother Teresa: The Life and Works of a Modern Saint* (New York: Time Books, 2010), 37. (5) "Quotes about the cross," Goodreads.com, accessed March 1, 2013, http://www.goodreads.com/quotes/tag?id=cross&page=2&utf8=%E2%9C%93.

Impressions

The Rescue

The following poem was written by one of our sword sisters. May it inspire you, too, to wake up and take up your sword.

The Rescue
By Gabrielle Kelley

Deep in slumber, I had a dream
About a Beautiful little girl,
Carefree and happy,
Running, jumping, laughing,
  and playing.

I awakened feeling joyful,
Reminded of my own childhood.
I remembered those carefree days
And sweetly fell back to sleep.

Again I saw this Beautiful little girl,
But something was terribly wrong.
Her father was handing her over
To a man with sinister eyes and
  an evil smile.

In exchange for a stack of bills,
The little girl was sold.
Taken away from childhood
And betrayed by her family.

I woke up once more,
This time disturbed and scared.
Down to the depths of my soul
I mourned for the girl in my
  dream.

"God, why am I dreaming about
Such a horrible, tragic thing?"
"Go back to sleep, child."
So I lay my head down and
  drifted...off...

Again in the land of dreams
I saw a large valley
Dotted with trees and bushes,
Rocks and streams.

I scanned the horizon.
Something dark and dank
Caught my attention:
A menacing cave scarring the
  valley's edge.

I looked harder and as I did
I saw a trembling figure in
  the cave.
It was the Beautiful Girl
Weeping quietly into her hands.

Her body was covered in bruises.
Her eyes were swollen and red.
Blood stained the floor beneath her.
And her clothes were covered in
  dirt and tears.

A big man walked into the cave,
Forced her onto her dirty mattress.
And then...well...
Some things are unspeakable.

Deeply shaken,
I sat straight up in bed
Panting and crying,
Sweating and trembling.

I knew that this wasn't a dream.
I knew in my spirit
That the girl was real…
And she was waiting for *me* to
    rescue her.

I jumped out of bed,
Flung open my closet doors,
And looked for something
To wear into battle.

There before me hung a
Gleaming coat of armor,
Strung with metal links, yes,
But also covered in rubies and
    sapphires.

Above it rested a helmet of gold,
Beautifully crafted and molded.
I quickly dressed.
Everything was a perfect fit.

As I placed a pair of sturdy leather
    boots
Upon my feet,
I spotted a sword and sheath,
Which I strapped to my side.

I turned around,
Amazed by my armor,
And caught a glimpse of myself
In my bedroom mirror.

I froze as a flame filled my heart
And a Presence filled the room.
I felt strength enter my arms
And purpose ignite my soul.

Emblazoned on my helmet,
Lit by the Presence, I read:
*"DELIVERER. SPEAKING
    FOR THOSE
WHO CANNOT SPEAK FOR
    THEMSELVES."*

Upon my armor was written:
*"BEAUTIFUL RESCUE.
RECLAIMING THOSE
    WHO ARE
STUMBLING TOWARD
    SLAUGHTER."*

At the edges of my ankles,
    illuminated words:
*"CONQUEROR OF DARKNESS,
PRESENTER OF PEACE,
HOPE FOR THE HOPELESS."*

Upon the sheath of my sword,
Glowing brighter than the rest,
Was written:
"FEAR NO EVIL."

And finally, pulling out my sword,
Glimmering in the Light of the
    Presence, the words:
*"THE LORD YOUR GOD
    WILL BE WITH YOU
WHEREVER YOU GO."*

My heart couldn't have beaten
more wildly.
My body couldn't have felt lighter.
My spirit couldn't have been stronger.
I was ready to go.

Knowing I had all I needed,
I ran down the steps,
Sprang through the door…
And stopped dead in my tracks.

There before me stood
The most beautiful, black Steed
That I have ever seen,
Even in my dreams.

He was fitted for a journey:
A beautiful saddle,
A gleaming bridle,
And a look of determination
in his eyes.

As I approached him I noticed
There was something written on
his forehead:
"ZEAL!
TO GOD BE THE GLORY."

I knew this was my mount.
Here was the means for my journey
To the rescue of
The Beautiful little girl.

I jumped onto the Steed's back,
Placed the reins in my hands
And whispered in his ear,
"Let's go."

As if waiting for that command,
The Steed bolted forward,
Down the street, past darkened
buildings…
And toward the valley.

As we neared the valley,
I recognized it.
Incredibly, it was the same valley
As the one in my dream.

However, mingled among the
rocks,
The streams, the trees and bushes,
Dark figures were crouched.
My heart began to melt with
trepidation.

Then the face of the Beautiful
little girl
Entered my mind
Giving me the strength to press
forward,
Whatever the threat.

As soon as I entered the valley
I heard a deep rolling battle cry
Plowing like thunder
Up and down the ravine.

It was not inspiring.
It was not invigorating.
It was not the battle cry of Good.
No, it was the battle cry of
Darkness and Evil.

A shiver went down my spine
And goosebumps covered my arms.
What had I gotten myself into?
How could I face this Dark Army
    alone?

But there was no time to think.
The Dark Ones swarmed toward me
Like so many black bees,
All of them intently looking into
    my eyes.

There was nothing to do but pray.
"Oh God of the Angel Armies!
Deliver me!
Help me to fight through this sinister
    horde!"

Suddenly a figure appeared,
Treading softly by my side.
I glanced over to see
A beautiful, radiant Lion.

I knew not who He was,
But with Light like that
He must be on my side.
He was there to help me fight.

With a newfound courage
And the Lion by my side
I picked up my speed
And headed into my Destiny.

The angry mob of Dark Ones
Drew nearer and nearer.
My breath quickened,
But my purpose remained sure:

I must fight through them.
I must reach the other side of the
    valley
And rescue the Beautiful little girl.
Or I must die trying.

The clash of sword against sword
Vibrated through my entire body.
I leaned down and with all my
    strength
Defeated the first Dark One who
    approached me.

Again and again this happened
And I began to get dizzy with
    the fight,
Overwhelmed with the sheer
    amount
Of those who were against me.

My eyes began to droop
And my arms felt heavy with
    exhaustion.
I was losing hope
And giving in to defeat.

Just as I was about to fall from
    my saddle,
About to succumb to the strength
    of the Darkness,
I felt a hot breath on my cheek,
And heard a growl in my ear.

It was the Lion.
"Don't give up, Warrior Princess,
    my Lioness,"
He said in a whisper as soft as a kiss
And as frightening as a roar.

With these words
A fresh wind entered my bones
And a new determination
Filled my heart.

An image of the Beautiful little girl,
Crying and desperate for rescue,
Flashed in my mind.
I could not give up on her.

She was all alone.
She was battered and bruised.
And the Lion and I,
We were the only ones in the valley
    fighting for her.

We picked up our pace
As a scream pierced our ears.
It was the Beautiful little girl,
"Please, someone help me!"

"We're coming!" I cried.
"Don't lose hope, little one!
You are not alone!
You are not forgotten!"

I don't think she could hear me,
But in my heart I prayed
That she wouldn't give up,
That she would stay strong just a
    little while longer.

Then a Dark One, bigger than I,
Barreled toward me,
Stopping me in my tracks
And leaving me nowhere to turn.

"The Beautiful little girl is mine.
I have claimed her for my
    Dark ways.
She is easy money
And guilty pleasure.

I will not let you pass.
I will not let you rescue her.
She belongs to the Darkness now,
And I care not about her pitiful
    fate."

I burned with anger.
Consumed with this righteous
    wrath,
The Steed and I galloped toward
    him,
The sword of **NO FEAR** pointed
    at his throat.

But he was bigger, stronger,
Quicker than I.
With the butt of his sword
He knocked me to the ground.

"This is the end," I thought.
"I have done all I can.
The Beautiful little girl must live
    alone,
Destined to this cruel fate."

As my heart broke with sadness
A sudden ear-splitting roar
Broke through the air.
Of course…The Lion was still
    here!

His big, beautiful, golden body
Leapt through the air.
With Holy Anger in His eyes,
He jumped upon the Dark One.

Injured but alive,
I stood to my feet,
And ran toward the pile of
Golden fur enfolding the Darkness.

The Dark One was defeated,
But to my dismay,
The Lion was bleeding
From a fatal wound in His side.

Struggling for breath,
He said to me,
"Do not fear. Death is defeated.
The Beautiful little girl's
deliverance is at hand."

As He breathed His last,
A river of blood streamed from
　His side.
As the river flowed,
I saw the message written within it:

"WONDERFUL LOVE," it said.
Then I knew who this Lion was.
He had not only died for the
　Beautiful little girl's rescue…
But for mine as well.

And with that death,
He commissioned me
To walk in the way of Him who
　shed His blood
For the redemption and rescue of
　His beloved ones.

The fight continued,
It lasted for what seemed an age.
I ran and fought and pushed on
For the Love of the Lion and His
　Beautiful little girl.

The going was not easy,
But I wouldn't have wanted to be
Anywhere but there in that valley,
Battling for Love,
　WONDERFUL LOVE.

The Lion was gone,
But His Presence was still with me,
Somehow stronger and more real
Than the Lion Himself had been.

His strength filled my soul.
His courage enveloped my spirit.
His passion coursed through
　my veins.
And His Love filled my heart.

I became scratched and bruised.
But He kept me going.
I was taunted and jeered.
But His Truths were all I listened to.

I was told to give up, that I would
　never succeed,
But His promises remained my
　anthem.
I was laughed at and scorned,
But I just kept going because I
　knew He was with me.

As I continued to fight I realized,
There is nothing more glorious,
More fulfilling, more incredible,
Than going into battle with and
    for the King of Kings.

Just as I was beginning to think
The battle would last eternally,
The air became quiet
And the clash of steel ceased.

I looked around me.
I was alone.
The Dark Ones had all fled or died.
And I stood right in front of the cave.

I couldn't believe my eyes.
There she was in front of me:
The Beautiful little girl all this
    fighting had been for,
Still broken and crying on the
    dirty ground.

I jumped off the Steed.
I ran to her side.
I placed my hand gently on her
    head, and whispered,
"You are free."

Timidly she looked up and said in
    a cracked voice,
"Free? How could I be free?
I was sold and betrayed
And they have enslaved me forever."

"No, dear one.
Not forever.
WONDERFUL LOVE
Was coming to rescue you all along."

"Why would anyone want to rescue
    me?
I am wretched, broken, and dirty.
Why would anyone fight for me?
How could someone care for such
    a tarnished little girl?"

Just then, the Lion, glowing with
    the Presence,
Appeared at the mouth of the cave,
And said,
**"Because you are My Jewel,
    My Beloved."**

Tears escaped from the Beautiful
    little girl's eyes
And streamed down her cheeks.
She ran toward the Lion
And buried her face in His mane.

I cried, too, knowing this was all
For His glory, for His fame,
For His Kingdom and for His
    honor.
How privileged I was to be a part
    of this miracle.

"I place her in your care,"
The Lion said to me.
Then He roared a glorious roar
    and was gone,
Leaving the Presence, the girl,
    and me, behind.

I wrapped the Beautiful Girl in
    my arms.
I washed her face and tended to
    her wounds.

I took her out of the valley and
brought her home.
And I reminded her that she is
Loved.

This is my reason for living:
To go to battle against the powers
of Darkness.
To seek out those condemned to
death
And to risk it all to rescue them.

I know the valleys are real.
What's worse, so are the caves.
The girls within are crying out
to us,
And we are responsible for their
rescue.

Does the Word not say,
"Rescue those being
Led away to death; hold back those
Staggering toward slaughter.

If you say, 'But we knew nothing
about this,'
Does not He who weighs the heart
perceive it?
Does not He who guards your heart
know it?
Will He not repay each person
according to what he has done?"
(Proverbs 24:11-12, NIV)

God opened my eyes.
He let me see and learn about
the caves,
The Darkness,
And the girls.

I cannot ignore their cries.
I cannot live my life for myself.
Pretending that the Beautiful little
girls don't exist,
Or that someone else will rescue
them.

I have to do my part.
I'm not totally sure what that
means.
But I'm determined to figure
it out,
With the help of the Lion.

Here I am, Lord.
I'll ride into battle with You
And claim the ones You have
chosen…
Because of Your
WONDERFUL LOVE.

Amen.

GIRLS WITH SWORDS

HOW TO CARRY YOUR CROSS LIKE A HERO

CURRICULUM

Curriculum Includes:

- ⚜ 8 video sessions on 3 DVDs
  (30 minutes each)
- ⚜ 8 audio sessions on 4 CDs
  (30 minutes each)
- ⚜ *Girls with Swords* hardcover book
- ⚜ Fencing Manual
- ⚜ Sword necklace: Gold plated with 18-inch chain
- ⚜ Promotional materials

Churches & Pastors

Local churches are the passion and heart of this ministry. Our Church Relations team connects with pastors, churches, and ministry leaders worldwide. It is their joy and honor to encourage leaders, pray for churches, provide life-transforming resources, and build authentic relationships.

UNITED STATES	AUSTRALIA	UNITED KINGDOM
1-800-648-1477	1-300-650-577	0800-9808-933

LIONESS ARISING

Wake Up and Change Your World

Curriculum Includes:

- 8 sessions on 3 DVDs and 4 CDs (30 minutes each)
- Hardcover book
- *Safari Guide* study guide
- Promotional materials

The lioness is a magnificent image of strength, passion, and beauty. Her presence commands the landscape, protects her young, and empowers the lion. Packed with remarkable insights from nature and a rich depth of biblical references to the lioness, *Lioness Arising* is a call for women to rise up in strength and number to change their world.

Curriculum Includes:

- 7 Sessions on 3 DVDs & 3 CDs (30 minutes each)
- *Nurture* Book
- Devotional Workbook
- Encouraging Videos from 17 international leaders
- Promotional Materials
- Cross Necklace: Adjustable 16-18 inch Genuine Swarovski Crystal Necklace

nurture

Give and Get What You Need to Flourish

Nurture is what you need to give and get! As God's daughters, it is our season to flourish! This curriculum positions you to make connections, write your life, reclaim your feminine intuition, strengthen your family, and find your place as the world-changer God has destined you to be.

Beautiful Daughter, this world needs you, so find your voice and bring your strength!

Fight Like *a Girl*
The Power of Being a Woman

You are an answer, not a problem.

Curriculum Includes:

- 12 Video Sessions on 4 DVDs (30 minutes each)
- *Fight Like a Girl* Book
- Devotional Workbook
- Promotional Materials & Bookmark
- Makeup Bag
- Bracelet – Genuine Swarovski Austrian Crystal

In *Fight Like a Girl*, Lisa challenges the status quo that a woman needs to fit into the role of a man, and she leads you in the truth of what it means to be a woman. Discover how to express your God-given strengths and fulfill your role in the community, workplace, home, and church. This curriculum will encourage you to find your true potential and realize you are an answer and not a problem.

THE KISSED GIRLS AND MADE THEM CRY

Curriculum Includes:

- 4 Video Sessions & Bonus Q&A on 2 DVDs (50-60 minutes each)
- Best-selling Book
- Devotional Workbook
- Promotional Materials

Don't believe the lie—sexual purity isn't about rules...it's about freedom and power. It is time to take back what we've cheaply given away. This kit is for women of all ages who long for a greater intimacy with Jesus and need to embrace God's healing and restoring love.

"I'm 15, and through your kit my nightmare has been turned back to a dream!"

additional RESOURCES

Life Without Limits – DVD

It is definitely no longer about us, but about Him! God is calling a generation of women who are willing to take risks and go out over their heads in Him. Women brave enough to trust Him with every area of their lives. He is watching for wild women who will be reckless in both their abandonment to God and their commitment to obedience. It is time to embrace His freedom in every area. This powerful and dynamic video was recorded at a women's mentoring conference and will empower you in these crucial areas:

- Completing versus competing
- Making your marriage a place of power
- Refining and defining your motivation
- Harnessing your power of influence
- Answering the mandate

Healing for the Angry Heart – 4 CD SET

In *Healing for the Angry Heart*, author Lisa Bevere provides practical, biblical insights to help you deal with the past and move forward in your life.

In this course, Lisa discusses:

- Her Anger Issues
- The Power of Confession
- Stopping Anger Before It Gets Out of Hand
- Letting It Go
- Putting It Into Practice
- Anger and Depression
- Anger and Fear

The Power of Two with One Heart – CD

God never intended our marriages to be something we endure, but a beautiful and exciting haven where both the man and woman flourish.

In *The Power of Two with One Heart*, Lisa calls out to both men and women to see God's original plan for marriage and to take back what has been lost. When we embrace our roles and lend our strengths, it is then the restoration can begin.

With God, it's always been about one man, one woman, one heart.

Extreme Makeover – 2 CD SET

Makeovers of every kind are the current craze. Not only are faces and bodies being overhauled, but everything is subject to this before-and-after experimentation. People just can't seem to get enough, and rather than judging, the church needs to ask the all-important question...Why? I believe it is because we are all desperate for change!

It's Time – CD

For too long we have had the attitude, "It's my turn!" But when God begins to pour out His Spirit, it is nobody's turn; it becomes every-body's time. It is time for God's gifts in His body to come forth. The Father is gifting men and women alike to shine in each and every realm of life. Discover what He has placed in your hand and join the dance of a lifetime.